TOPICS IN APPLIED GEOGRAPHY

TOURIST DEVELOPMENT

TOPICS IN APPLIED GEOGRAPHY
edited by Donald Davidson and John Dawson

Douglas G. Pearce
University of Canterbury
Christchurch
New Zealand

Elaine Crichton
November
1983.

TOURIST DEVELOPMENT

Longman
London
and New York

Longman Group Limited
Longman House
Burnt Mill, Harlow, Essex, UK

Published in the United States of America
by Longman Inc., New York

© Longman Group Limited 1981

First published 1981

British Library Cataloguing in Publication Data

Pearce, Douglas G.
  Tourist development. – (Topics in applied
geography)
  1. Tourist trade
  I. Title   II. Series
  338.4'7'91   G155.A1

  ISBN 0-582-30053-3

Library of Congress Cataloguing in Publication Data

Pearce, Douglas G., 1949–
  Tourist development.

  (Topics in applied geography)
  Bibliography: p.
  Includes index.
  1. Tourist trade. I. Title. II. Series.
  G155.A1P36   380.1'459104   81-3717
  ISBN 0-582-30053-3   AACR2

Printed in Great Britain by
William Clowes (Beccles) Ltd
Beccles and London

CONTENTS

LIST OF FIGURES

LIST OF TABLES

ACKNOWLEDGEMENTS

Parts of Chapter 6 draw on research supported by the New Zealand National Commission for UNESCO and the Department of Lands and Survey, Wellington, whose assistance is gratefully acknowledged.

My thanks go to Bob Mings and Barry Johnston for their constructive comments after reviewing a first draft of the manuscript; to John Dawson for editorial advice; to Sue Cooper and Anna Moloney for typing the manuscript, and to Alastair Dyer who drafted the maps and diagrams. Special thanks to Chantal for her support and encouragement.

Doug Pearce
Christchurch
October, 1980.

and 6.2 from 'A Case Study of Queenstown' pp. 23–45 in *Tourism and the Environment*, Department of Land Survey, Wellington 1978; University of Pennsylvania Press Fig. 1 p. 9 from 'Frequency of Types of Tourists and their adaptations to local Homes' and Peck and Lepie's 'Typology of Tourist Development' p. 160 – both in *Hosts and Guests: the Anthropology of Tourism* 1977; University of Wales Press for Table 3.3 'Tourist Income and Output Multipliers in Anglesey 1970 in *The Impact of Domestic Tourism* by B.H. Archer 1973; University of Waterloo, Ontario, for Fig. 8 'Impacts of Recreation on Wildlife' in *The Environmental Impact of Outdoor Recreation* by G. Wall and C. Wright (publication series No. 11) 1977; World Tourist Organization, Madrid, for Fig. of Le Plagne in Le Bulletin d'etudes touristiques de 1978 and Mission Interministerielle pour l'Amenagement Touristique du Littoral Languedoc–Roussillon, Paris for Table, p. 12, *France Languedoc–Roussillon: Information for Investors*.

CHAPTER 1
INTRODUCTION

Tourism has been defined in various ways but may be thought of as the relationships and phenomena arising out of the journeys and temporary stays of people travelling primarily for leisure or recreational purposes. The duration of these stays may vary. For statistical purposes, a four-night minimum is commonly accepted for domestic tourism but stays of only twenty-four hours are universally recognized in the case of international tourism. Some writers employ a minimum trip length but the critical factor is movement away from the place of permanent residence to the holiday destination or destinations. In certain cases, the holiday itself may consist of a single, continuous journey. Spatial interaction is thus an inherent feature of tourism and the subject lends itself readily to geographical analysis. The geography of tourism is concerned essentially, though not exclusively, with the spatial expression of the relationships and phenomena to which short-term leisure travel gives rise.

Geographers were first attracted to the study of tourism half a century ago. Early American geographers saw tourism as a distinct and significant form of land use (McMurray, 1930; Brown, 1935) and tended to concentrate on the economic aspects of tourism (Carlson, 1938). Other writers observed that tourism modified the existing landscape and gave rise to new and different urban forms (Jones, 1933; Eiselen, 1945). The main British contribution in this early period was Gilbert's work on the morphology of inland and seaside resorts (1939, 1949). In France Miège (1933) had provided a base for the many regional studies which were to follow later with his substantial discussion of tourism in Savoy. According to Miège, tourism had a two-fold interest for geographers, it involved the movement of people and constituted a regional resource. The most significant German pre-war study was by Poser (1939) who examined the distribution and locational attributes of various forms of tourism in the Reisengebirge.

Although these important foundations were laid before the war, it was not until the 1960s in Europe and the 1970s in North America and elsewhere that geographical studies of tourism started to appear frequently in the literature. At the same time, the subject was attracting increasing interest from a number of other disciplines, notably economics, business management, sociology and anthropology. In many respects this growing academic interest reflects the marked post-war expansion of tourism. The World Tourism Organization (WTO) estimates the number of international tourist arrivals in 1979 at about 275 million and receipts from international tourism at about 75 billion dollars. By some definitions international tourism is second only to oil as the single largest item of world trade. To this can be added the domestic tourism component which, according to the WTO, accounts for four times as many movements as international tourism.

Even though an increasing number of researchers from various branches of geography have examined different facets of tourism, a cohesive body of knowledge and methodology which might be thought of as the geography of tourism has been slow to emerge (Pearce, 1979a). Nevertheless, six broad topic areas can be thought of as constituting the major components of the geography of tourism:

1. Spatial patterns of supply.
2. Spatial patterns of demand.
3. The geography of resorts.
4. Tourist movements and flows.
5. The impact of tourism.
6. Models of tourist space.

The study of tourist development spans all these areas but is concerned primarily with supply, resorts and the impact of tourism.

TOURIST DEVELOPMENT

Tourist development might be defined specifically as the provision or enhancement of facilities and services to meet the needs of the tourist. More generally, it might also include associated impacts such as employment creation or income generation.

Tourist development takes many forms. Classic examples include coastal, thermal or alpine resorts such as Benidorm, Bath and Chamonix. On a different scale, Tokyo, London and Paris each year attract millions of tourists who must be catered for. Then there is the second home phenomenon, be this in the form of converted farm cottages in the Auvergne or massive condominium construction in Colorado. The building of Disneyland and the opening of British stately homes or Canadian national parks to the public, together with their conservation measures, constitute other forms of tourist development. Often less apparent alongside hotels, restaurants, marinas and ski-fields is an accompanying infrastructure – airports, motorways, sewage treatment plants – which may be developed wholly or partly to serve the travelling public. Moreover, all these different developments can occur in different ways, at different scales and at different rates.

Tourist development also takes place in many different contexts. Modern mass tourism has its origins in the affluence of the industrialized nations of Western Europe, North America and, more recently, Japan. Tourism has also expanded significantly in Eastern Europe and is becoming an important sector in many developing countries in Asia, Africa, Latin America, the Pacific and the Caribbean. Thus tourism has developed in liberal Western societies, under highly planned socialist regimes, as a relatively small part of large industrial economies or again as the leading sector of small developing countries. Likewise, tourism has developed in a wide variety of physical environments – on low islands of the Pacific, in the heart of Alpine Europe, in the countryside of the English Lakes District and along the Mediterranean coastline.

As a result, the form tourist development may take can vary enormously from situation to situation, from one context to another. There is no more any one type of tourist development than there is a single model of agricultural, industrial or urban growth. However, this has been ignored by many writers, particularly those examining the social or cultural impact of tourist development. Summing up the 1976 symposium on tourism and culture change held by the American Anthropological Association, Nash (cited by Smith, 1977a, p. 133) noted: 'In these papers generally, the causal agent (tourism or some aspect of tourism) tends not to be well delineated or explicated. We have to dig to find out what it is.' At the same time it is possible to identify the various factors involved in tourist development and to describe general relationships among them. That is the aim of this book, to examine tourist development systematically in order to provide the reader with a general appreciation of the subject and a basic framework and methodology with which he may then address particular problems. The aim is not so much to provide the technical details for the planner (cf. Lawson and Baud-Bovy, 1977) but rather to present a general overview of tourist development, outlining the different factors involved and emphasizing the nature of the relationships between them.

The spatial dynamics of tourist space

A useful starting point for a systematic analysis of tourist development is found in Miossec's model of the spatial dynamics of tourist space (Fig. 1.1). In determining the structural evolution of tourist regions through time and space, Miossec (1976; 1977) considers four basic elements: (1) resorts; (2) transport networks; (3) the behaviour of tourists; and (4) the attitudes of the local decision-makers and population. As the tourist industry expands an increasingly complex hierarchical system of resorts and transport networks evolves, the tourists become more aware of the region's possibilities with consequent changes in their behaviour. Changes in local attitudes may lead to the complete acceptance of tourism, the adoption of planning controls or even the rejection of tourism.

As a general framework of tourist development, Miossec's model contains several useful points. Firstly, it embodies a dynamic element, the development of the region through time and space. This notion of spatial/temporal evolution is critical, both in analysing past processes and in planning the path future development is to take. Secondly, it attempts an overview of this evolution; changes in the behaviour of the tourists and the local population are related to the growth of resorts and the expansion of the transport network. However, as Miossec notes, each of the four elements need not develop apace and therein lies the source of many of the problems to which tourism may give rise. The key factor is that impact is related to development, and more importantly, particular impacts are related to specific stages of development. Other aspects of the development process are less explicit although they might be incorporated into the model. Some activities are attributed to the local population, for example the provision of supplies and the development of infrastructure, but the actual means of and the agents for development are not elaborated on. Who builds the resorts, how, for what reasons and with what results are fundamental questions which must be asked and answered. Likewise, the factors which influence the location of the resorts and the form of the hierarchies which emerge must also be examined. More generally, the context in which this development takes place is also neglected.

Miossec's model highlights the geographer's interest in tourist development and the applied contribution he might make in this field. Clearly there is a significant spatial element in the organization and planning of tourism. More generally, an understanding of tourist development processes will lead to a greater awareness and fuller comprehension of how places change or might be changed as tourism is established or expands. Given the recent growth of the industry in many parts of the world, such an appreciation is becoming increasingly important not only to geographers but also to planners, local authorities and government agencies as well as to the populations of the host communities.

Building on the basic framework provided by Miossec's model, Chapter 2 examines in more detail the various elements involved in tourist development and outlines the roles and functions of the various agents of development. These elements and agents are then drawn together in a discussion of various classifications of tourist development. The third chapter analyses the factors influencing the distribution of facilities and site selection before discussing methods of assessing tourist potential. A general framework for assessing the impact of tourism is presented in Chapter 4, and followed by a discussion of the more specific economic, social and environmental impacts which tourism may have and the means of

RESORTS phases	TRANSPORT phases	TOURIST BEHAVIOR phases	ATTITUDES OF DECISION MAKERS AND POPULATION OF RECEIVING REGION phases
0 A B territory traversed distant	0 transit isolation	0 ? lack of interest and knowledge	0 A B mirage refusal
1 pioneer resort	1 opening up	1 global perception	1 observation
2 multiplication of resorts	2 increase of transport links between resort	2 progress in perception of places and itineraries	2 infrastructure policy servicing of resorts
Organisation of the holiday space of each resort. Beginning of a hierarchy and specialisation.	Excursion circuits	Spatial competition and segregation	segregation demonstration effects dualism
hierarchy specialisation saturation	connectivity → maximum	Disintegration of perceived space. Complete humanization. Departure of certain types of tourists. Forms of substitution. Saturation and crisis	A B total tourism development plan ecological safeguards

1.1 A synthesis of the dynamics of tourist space.
(Miossec 1976)

evaluating these. In the light of these impacts and the processes outlined earlier, Chapter 5 considers planning for tourist development at the national, regional and local levels. Throughout these chapters general points and principles will be illustrated by reference to specific examples. In Chapter 6 an overview is attempted, drawing these various threads together in two more detailed and comprehensive case studies. The first concerns the recent and largely unplanned evolution of a New Zealand resort, Queenstown. The second discusses planned development on a regional scale, using the example of Languedoc-Roussillon in Southern France. Conclusions are then drawn.

CHAPTER 2
STRUCTURES AND PROCESSES OF TOURIST DEVELOPMENT

Tourist development embraces the provision of a wide range of facilities and services. This chapter examines the spectrum of supply, considers the roles and functions of the various development agents then brings the two together in a discussion of typologies of development. Although by no means exhaustive, this structured examination aims to provide a general basis for analysing tourist development.

ELEMENTS OF SUPPLY

The numerous types of facilities and services sought by the tourist can be grouped into the following broad sectors:

1. Attractions;
2. Transport;
3. Accommodation;
4. Supporting facilities;
5. Infrastructure.

The attractions induce the tourists to visit the area, transport services enable him to do so, the accommodation and supporting facilities (e.g. shops, restaurants) cater for his well-being while there and the infrastructure assures the essential functioning of all of these.

From a development point of view, these facilities and services can be classified into three further categories, depending on whether they are purpose-built, transformed or shared with other activities. Facilities built expressly for tourism range from attractions such as Disneyland to resort hotels to ski-field access roads. Others have been transformed from their original function to some tourist use, for example farm cottages have become second homes, and old canals and waterways have been restored for recreational boating. In other instances, tourism may supplement the original activity – wine-makers have opened their cellars to tourists and Gothic cathedrals today attract the curious as much as the faithful. Or, tourists may share their accommodation and transport with other travellers and take advantage of services and infrastructure provided essentially for the resident population.

Attractions

Many different attractions may induce tourists to visit particular areas or spend their holidays in specific regions. These have been classified in a variety of ways (Suzuki, 1967;

Peters, 1969; Defert, 1972). A first distinction is usually made between natural features such as land forms, flora and fauna and man-made objects, historic or modern, in the form of cathedrals, casinos, monuments, historic buildings or amusement parks. A third general category embraces man and his culture as expressed through language, music, folklore, dances, cuisine and so forth. More specific attractions and means of evaluating them are discussed in Chapter 3.

Transport

Historically, the development of tourism has been closely associated with advances in transport technology. The early development of spas and seaside resorts depended largely on the development of the railways. In the post-war period, the rapid rise in automobile ownership has been responsible for the vast increase in domestic tourism in Western societies and improved aircraft technology has led to a boom in international travel. However, in addition to increasing the volume of tourist traffic, these advances in transportation have also modified the patterns of tourist flows and hence the patterns of development (Fig. 2.1). Lundgren (1972) and Rajotte (1975) note how travel patterns have become much more flexible and diffuse, with the ubiquitous automobile replacing the linearly constrained railways or river steamers.

Studies of the period, such as those by Carlson (1938) and Deasy (1949), also show the effect that the motor car was beginning to have on travel patterns and the rise and fall in the popularity of destinations and types of accommodation. In particular, development was spread beyond those localities served by the traditional means of transport. Large terminus hotels, for example, gave way to highway cabins and eventually to motels. However,

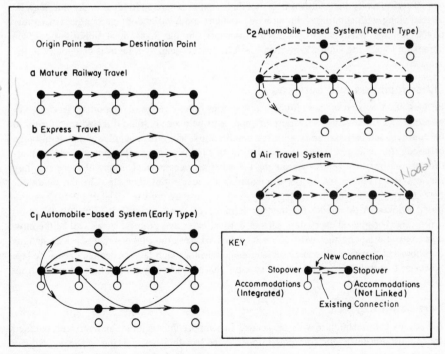

2.1 The evolution of tourist travel systems.
     (Lundgren, 1972)

Lundgren (Fig. 2.1) also suggests that the subsequent construction of major highway networks has again 'canalized' travellers by the superior accessibility they provide. The modern air-based travel system is nodal in nature and the high levels of technology and capital required favour a metropolitan-based dominance of the system.

Accommodation

Many different forms of accommodation are available to the modern tourist. These might be broadly classified into the commercial sector (hotels, motels, boarding houses, holiday camps, etc.) and the private sector, notably private permanent residences used for hosting friends and relations and second homes (defined by Downing and Dower (cited by Coppock, 1977, p. 3) as: 'a property owned or rented on a long lease as the occasional residence of a household that usually lives elsewhere'). Camping and caravanning may constitute an intermediate category wherein private tents or caravans are sited in commercial camping grounds. Certain holiday communities may consist primarily of second homes and luxury hotels may form the basis of select isolated resorts but most destinations will offer a mix of accommodation types, the mix depending on the nature of the resort and its clientele.

In general, there has been a move away from the traditional serviced type of accommodation provided by hotels and guest houses to more flexible and functional forms such as the self-contained motel or the rented apartment. Flexibility in ownership is also apparent. Resort apartments in France may be purchased completely, under a variety of lease-back arrangements, or, more recently, on a time-sharing basis whereby a series of owners acquire rights to a property for specified periods of the year. Various collective types of accommodation have also emerged in Europe, particularly in association with policies of social tourism. These usually take the form of holiday camps, where individual bedrooms may be offered along with communal dining halls, lounges and a variety of entertainment or recreational facilities. Many such facilities are sponsored by the State, local authorities or trade unions, although the Club Méditerranée with its pseudo-native villages is essentially of the same format.

Other facilities and services

Besides the provision of these immediate facilities quite a range of supporting services will be required by the tourist. A variety of shops will be needed, some oriented specifically to the tourist, such as souvenir or sporting goods shops, and others supplying a general range of goods; for example, chemists, foodstores or clothing shops. Restaurants, banks, hairdressers and medical centres are among the other services needed. Many of these auxiliary services and facilities may serve a predominantly residential clientele. The thresholds for services vary according to the frequency with which they are used. Defert (1966) has proposed a hierarchical model for the development of these services in a traditional resort (Fig. 2.2). Those used every day, such as dairies, cafes and grocers' stores will be the most numerous and among the first to be established whereas the higher order services such as jewellers and furriers will come at a later stage when a much larger clientele exists. Today, however, resort development may be so rapid that some luxury services are provided from the outset.

Infrastructure

An adequate infrastructure will be needed to support the facilities and services outlined above. In addition to the transport infrastructure (roading and parking, airfields, railway lines, harbours) there are the public utilities in the form of electricity and sewage disposal. Much of this infrastructure will also serve the resident population or other needs (e.g.

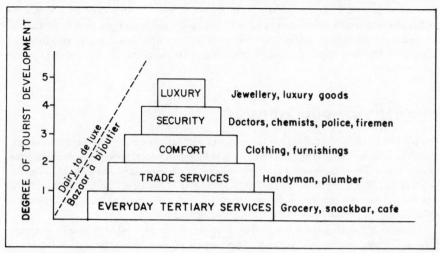

2.2 Development of shops and services in a tourist resort.
(After Defert, 1966)

agricultural) but, depending on the type of development, it may also be developed, or expanded, expressly for the tourist. The critical point regarding infrastructure is that although it is essential it is basically a charge on development. With a few exceptions, such as toll-roads, the infrastructure does not itself generate revenue directly. There is little money to be made from disposing of sewage and failure to provide adequate treatment facilities has given rise to one of the more common adverse impacts of tourist development as numerous examples throughout the world testify.

Table 2.1 indicates the relative investment costs of these different sectors. Although the investment for each sector will vary from project to project, accommodation and infrastructure will normally necessitate the heaviest outlays.

Successful tourist development depends in large part on maintaining an adequate mix, both within and between these sectors. Natural or historical attractions might be complemented by purpose-built man-made ones to broaden the appeal of the resort or to capitalize on the existing market (apres-ski entertainment at ski-fields, the lions of Longleat or the wax museums at the Niagara Falls). A range of accommodation at a resort will reduce dependence on a single market. The balance between sectors can be expressed in terms of quality and quantity. Provision of top-grade accommodation at a mediocre attraction, for example, is unlikely to prove viable. Unless certain facilities are to be over-charged or under-utilized, the capacity of each of the sectors must be comparable, taking into account,

Table 2.1 Capital costs in tourist development (Lawson and Baud-Bovy, 1977, p. 21)

SECTOR	AVERAGE PROPORTIONS (%)
Accommodation and catering	50–60
Other tourist facilities	10–15
Technical and service infrastructures	15–20
Vocational training promotion, publicity	5–10
Protection and enhancement of resources	5–10

of course, the extent of non-tourist use. In respect to use it is important to note that the tourist product, unlike most others, cannot be stockpiled and resold at a later date. There is no market for last night's unsold hotel bed or yesterday's unoccupied plane seat. Balanced development through time and space is also critical. These points are developed in subsequent chapters.

AGENTS OF DEVELOPMENT

For tourism to develop, the various components outlined above must be exploited or supplied by someone or some organization. A wide range of development agents exists. The exact composition of these will vary from situation to situation, depending on the historical, political, economic, cultural and geographical context of the development. In general, we can distinguish between the public and private sectors and examine their participation at different levels: international, national, regional and local.

Central or federal government in most countries is complemented by smaller territorial local authorities (boroughs, counties). An intermediate tier of government also exists in many countries, such as the State and provincial governments in North America and the départements in France. Moreover, central government consists of a number of different agencies or departments, many of which may be involved in a tourist development programme. Their various activities may be co-ordinated by some national tourism organization. The participation of these different levels of government will depend on the nature and scale of the project but it would not be uncommon for all three levels to be represented in some way in a particular programme. In addition, particularly in the developing countries, international organizations, such as agencies of the United Nations, the World Bank, PATA, or the Organization of American States, may be actively involved in development.

Similar levels of operation are also evident in the private sector. Many of the largest tourist development companies will be engaged in tourist activities throughout the country. Others will limit their activities to particular regions and the smallest to local projects. Individual participation is most apparent at the local and regional levels. At the other extreme, multinational companies operate in a number of countries, most often the tourist generating ones as well as the destinations.

The involvement of these different bodies will depend on their motives, responsibilities and their capabilities.

Motives and responsibilities

Public sector

Economic. Various economic factors may induce the public sector to foster tourist development:

(a) improved balance of payments situation;
(b) regional development;
(c) diversification of the economy;
(d) increased income levels;
(e) increased State revenue (taxes);
(f) new employment opportunities.

Such factors may lead the public sector to participate directly in the development process. Central government may also have a responsibility to facilitate and stimulate private sector participation in an effort to promote economic growth. This will involve varying degrees of planning and co-ordination (Wolfson, 1967), the extent of public intervention being determined to a large degree by the philosophy of the government in question. However, in most, though not all, contexts, it will be the government's function to provide much of the necessary infrastructure.

Social.   Social considerations are also important. On the one hand there may be the objective to provide adequate recreational facilities for the nation's people. This has given rise to a policy of 'social tourism' in many European countries (Lanquar and Raynouard, 1978). On the other, there is a general responsibility to protect the social and economic well-being of the individual.

Environmental.   The responsibility of protecting and conserving the environment, both physical and cultural, usually falls to the public sector although it might be argued that there is an individual or corporate responsibility here as well.

Political.   As international tourism involves the movement of people from country to country, governments may encourage the development of tourism to further political objectives. Cals (1974) suggests that the Spanish government encouraged tourist development amongst other things to broaden the political acceptance of Franco's regime. In Israel, the development of tourism has done much to stimulate political sympathy for that nation and to boost national morale (Stock, 1977a).

Economic motivation has been the most significant of these factors to date. This remains true of the developing countries but several writers suggest that social and environmental goals are becoming increasingly important in the more developed countries (ECE, 1976; AIEST, 1978).

Responsibility may vary with the level of government. The responsibility for drawing up legislation, for example health or safety regulations, may rest with the central government but it may be the task of the territorial local authority to enforce those regulations. Likewise, tourist development plans may be formulated by central government but executed by regional or local authorities.

Private sector

The private sector's prime concern is with profit-making, as the basic responsibility of the developer is to maximize returns to the shareholders. Even so, different economic motives can influence participation in tourist development. Tourism may represent a form of diversification, a spreading of risk. Tourist development may also complement a company's existing activities. Many early coastal resorts were developed by railway companies seeking to generate new business and such companies remain to the fore today in developing tourism in Japan (Yamamura, 1970). This complementary development may be labelled integration. Two general types of integration are recognized (Baretje and Defert, 1972; IUOTO, 1975). Horizontal integration involves expansion within the same sector, for example the development of hotel chains or airline networks. Vertical integration, on the other hand, concerns participation in two or more sectors of the industry, as when tour operators acquire interests in transport and accommodation. On a smaller scale, individuals may become involved in tourism merely to earn a living or in an attempt to better themselves.

At the same time, there appear to be many ventures not characterized by a sound economic rationale but influenced more by the whims of a managing director or an individual who is attracted by the apparent glamour of the industry, by the desire to create something or merely because of enthusiasm for skiing. The individual second-home owner will be motivated as much by the desire to fulfil his own leisure ambitions as to develop or acquire an investment. Social and environmental concern might also be expressed by the private sector, if only to ensure the long-term security of its economic investment or even to appease public opinion.

Capabilities

In general, the ability of these development agents will increase with their size and larger projects will demand greater resources, both technical and financial. National or international developers will have more resources at their disposal than smaller regional or local concerns. The installation of a few simple rope tows may be within the scope of local enterprise whereas the construction of an intensive network of chairlifts may require external support. Grouping, whether of individuals, companies or public agencies, will generally increase development capability. The availability of resources for tourism will also depend on the size of the economy and the stage of economic development of the area in question as well as on the demands being made from other sectors – for example, industry or agriculture – for such resources as manpower and capital. This is particularly significant in the case of developing or declining economies at whatever level. There, both suitably trained personnel and investment capital may be scarce.

Central and State governments have the ability to legislate and even local authorities may pass bye-laws. Such activity can both encourage and regulate tourist development. Central government can not only influence the foreign tourist traffic by migration regulations, promotion budgets or the adjustment of overseas exchange rates, but also set legal limits on the extent of foreign investment and the repatriation of capital. Fiscal grants, incentives or taxes can encourage or limit investment in tourism or channel it to certain localities. Conservation legislation can protect a nation's natural and historical heritage. Such measures may run counter to the short-term exploitation of these resources although contributing to the nation's and the tourist industry's well-being in the long run. In terms of physical development, the ability of the territorial local authority to issue or withhold building permits may be its most important function. At the same time, however, large national or multinational companies may have sufficient economic and political weight to effectively nullify these regulations or manipulate legislation to their advantage.

Development

Tourist development occurs when motivation is matched with capability to provide the facilities and services outlined earlier. However, to be successful, this activity must occur under certain conditions, particularly the existence of a potential market for the product being developed. That is, supply must be matched with demand whether this is latent or created; for example, through extensive promotion.

Given the range of supply elements and the host of development agents with their different motivations and capabilities, innumerable types of tourist development occur. Certain common relationships however can be recognized. Because of the scale and extent of development, provision of the infrastructure is a widely accepted task of public authorities. Exceptions occur nevertheless, as in New Zealand where most ski-field access roads have been built and are maintained by private developers. Likewise isolated resorts commonly provide their own sewage treatment plants. National airlines, because of the extent of the investment required, the public interest involved and their role as flag carriers, are commonly government owned and operated, although here too a large number of exceptions exist, particularly in North America. Preservation, conservation and enhancement of natural

and to a lesser extent historical attractions are a major concern of the public sector, expressed most notably in national parks. Although involved in all sectors, private enterprise has
been most active in the accommodation and supporting facilities sector and in providing
purpose-built attractions. Government-sponsored hotel chains, such as the THC (Tourist
Hotel Corporation) in New Zealand and the Paradores in Spain also exemplify State participation in these sectors.

Most development will consist of a mix, either structured or informal, of these different development agents. The degree of public/private participation will depend in large part
on the scale and the nature of the project, the stage of development and on the capabilities
of each plus government policy. According to Cazes (1978, pp. 82–3) we have passed
from the nineteenth century situation characterized by: 'a coagulation of individual actions,
more or less grouped' to a more systematic, quasi institutionalized organization in which
central government formulates the programme and develops the basic infrastructure, leaving private enterprise to undertake the superstructure, and associated services. However,
this is perhaps truer of Western Europe than North America. Depending on the political
structure, the local authorities will play a minor supporting role or intervene actively (Wackermann, 1978; Préau, 1980). Cazes also suggests that whatever the relative weight of the
different partners, there is a growing tendency towards spatially concentrated projects in
which the different partners are brought together in increasingly complex financial and legal
arrangements. However, less formal, unstructured development also continues.

The initiative may come from either the public or the private sector. Government at
any level may solicit private capital and development through the provision of infrastructure, a development plan and fiscal incentives. Or, local authorities may have to extend
their public utilities or modify their town plan in response to pressure from private developers. The degree of involvement of each sector may change through time (Pearce, 1980a).
Conflict occurs when the capabilities or motivations of the different bodies differ, when, for
example, local infrastructure can no longer cope with the increased demands placed upon it
or when local concerns are unable to compete effectively with external developers.

TYPOLOGIES OF TOURIST DEVELOPMENT

To date, few writers have tried to identify and classify different types or processes of tourist
development. Much of the literature is ideographic in nature, with few attempts being made
to compare case studies let alone generalize from them. The typologies that have been
proposed serve the useful purpose of highlighting the fact that different processes of tourist
development can and do occur. More importantly, the criteria used in deriving these
typologies can provide a useful means of analysing tourism in other situations, for as Préau
(1968, p. 139) points out: 'a rigorous classification is less important than an analytical
method of examining reality'. Although these criteria vary, the typologies generally take
into account the characteristics of the developers and the resource being developed, the
manner in which the resource is developed, the context of development and its spatial
organization.

Most typologies have been confined to local and regional developments in particular
environments. The first two typologies reviewed here consider coastal developments at
different scales (Barbaza, 1970; Peck and Lepie, 1977). A third typology (Préau, 1970)
concerns tourism in the French Alps while the fourth (Pearce, 1978a) suggests a more
general classification not restricted to any one environment, but based on the division of
responsibility in the development process. Finally, the core-periphery nature of much tourist development is examined, with reference in particular to tourism in the Third World.

Coastal tourism

Barbaza (1970) distinguishes three types of development along the Mediterranean–Black Sea coastline using the following criteria:

1. The size and extent of the existing population and the vitality and diversity of its activities before the introduction of tourism.
2. The spontaneous or planned nature of the tourist facilities provided.
3. The localized or extensive nature of the tourist area.

Spontaneous development: Costa Brava–Côte d'Azur

In both these cases, tourism developed spontaneously. Along the Côte d'Azur (French Riviera), tourism developed in two stages. The first was characterized by a winter influx of the well-to-do in the eighteenth and nineteenth centuries which gave rise to resorts such as Cannes and Nice and the construction of villas on the slopes backing the littoral. In a second period, after the Second World War, mass summer tourism developed. This was accompanied by a general movement downslope to the beach and by massive and anarchic ribbon development of the littoral between the existing urban centres.

A comparable rocky coastline with a limited hinterland is found on Spain's Costa Brava. The aristocratic phase of tourism was largely absent here, the region being one of small fishing ports, some agriculture and a little industry associated with cork. Such activities created little functional unity and few links were developed throughout the coast or with the inland cities. However, the coastline and climate were extremely attractive and this, coupled with the relatively cheap cost of living, led to an influx of summer tourists in the post-war period. Demand preceded supply however, the region being ill-equipped for such activities. In the race to develop, much construction was anarchic. Some planning measures were introduced but environmental degradation was not altogether unavoided. There was also a substantial spatial reorganization of the region. Tourist facilities developed the length of the coast, the infrastructure was modernized and links were developed not only with the larger region but also the rest of Spain and, to a certain extent, Europe itself. A certain functional unity emerged. Nevertheless, many of the traditional activities continue.

Tourist resorts resulting from a planned and localized development – the Black Sea Coast

Generally sandy, flat and low-lying, the Black Sea littoral of Romania and Bulgaria was dominated by three large ports (Constanza, Varna and Bourgas) with little population or activity outside these centres. In the post-war period, the socialist governments embarked on a programme of tourist expansion to improve the inflow of foreign exchange and to promote social tourism. The decision to develop tourism was a conscious, carefully calculated one (the market was analysed, the capacity of beaches assessed) preceding virtually any tourist activity. This, coupled with the collective ownership of the land and the State's role in financing, led to the rapid construction of large holiday complexes of 15,000 to 25,000 beds, such as Mamia in Romania and Zlatni Pjasac in Bulgaria. Functional and very localized, such resorts have scarcely had any effect on the previous organization of the region which continues to be dominated by the large ports.

Extensive development: Languedoc–Roussillon

A number of small local resorts developed on France's Languedoc-Roussillon coastline but prior to the massive development operation of the 1960s the tourist potential of the coastline was largely unexploited (see Ch. 6). Although the object of a development plan, the

Languedoc–Roussillon operation differs from the Black Sea projects in that the plan not only incorporates the construction of new functional complexes but also the expansion and redevelopment of existing centres. Moreover, these are linked together by the infrastructure which thus unifies the region.

Significant differences emerge in Barbaza's study. In the first case development is dictated by demand, in the two others by supply. In the Costa Brava example, it is a question of controlling rampant private development; in the other two, the State plays a vital role in developing 'ex nihilo' functional resorts. However, the private sector also takes a major part in Languedoc–Roussillon.

Table 2.2 Peck and Lepie's typology of tourist development (Peck and Lepie, 1977, p. 160)

RATE OF CHANGE	POWER BASIS	PAYOFFS AND TRADE-OFFS EFFECTS ON LIFE-STYLE OF COMMUNITY
Rapid growth	'Bedroom' communities. Summer residents. Specialized commerce. (Outside financing.)	Rapid change of local money. New power structure and economy
Slow growth	Individual developments Local ownership. Expanding local commerce (Local financing.)	Slow change of norms. Stable power structure. Expanding local economy.
Transient development	Pass-throughs. Weekenders. Seasonal entrepreneurs. (Local financing.)	Stable norms. Individual mobility within power structure and economy. Little overall change in local economy.

The only other attempt at classifying coastal tourist development appears to be that by Peck and Lepie (1977) whose typology was developed for a study of small coastal communities in North Carolina. Three major criteria were established:

1. The rate of development, encompassing both magnitude and speed.
2. The power basis, which includes land ownership, source of financing, local input and the relation of local traditions to the development projects.
3. The impact of the host communities as expressed in terms of 'payoffs' (e.g. benefits to the host culture) and 'tradeoffs' (primarily the social impact).

Using these criteria a three-fold typology was developed (Table 2.2) and illustrated by three North Carolina communities. Although the differences in the examples do not appear as pronounced as the typology suggests, this does, nevertheless, provide a useful framework for the study of tourist development. The rapprochement of the effects of tourism and the processes of tourist development is especially useful.

Alpine tourism

In a first classification of ski-field developing in the French Alps, Préau (1968) concluded that in any situation three sets of factors intervene:

1. The state of the local community when development begins – its size, its dynamism, its facilities.
2. The rhythm of development – whether this coincides or not with the growth possibilities of the local community.
3. The characteristics of the site and the technical and financial possibilities for developing it.

These ideas are developed in a second article (Préau, 1970) where he proposes two different scenarios for the development of tourism in Alpine areas (Fig. 2.3). Between these two extremes, Préau recognizes the existence of a number of intermediate situations.

Chamonix – nineteenth century

The first scenario refers to summer tourism in the nineteenth century. The diagram reads from the top to bottom and emphasizes local conditions and factors which have been modified by tourists discovering the attractions of the alpine environment. The local society adapts rather readily to a diffuse and easily accommodated tourist demand. Urban developers from outside the area play only a gradual and complementary role, providing, for example, large hotels or capital for a mountain railway. Tourism is an effective germ for further economic and social development and little by little provides the conditions for 'take-off' (Veyret-Vernet, 1972).

Les Belleville – 1970

A completely different process operates in this contemporary situation and the diagram reads from bottom to top. Development now begins with the image of a functional resort conceived by urban promoters. It is no longer the mountains as such which are being presented to the tourist but the developed facilities – apartments, ski-lifts and associated recreational equipment. The mountain is reduced to a technical analysis of its characteristics – capacity of the ski-field, construction possibilities, ease of access, etc. Given the scale of the operation, perhaps in the order of 5,000–10,000 beds, it is the finance, techniques and knowhow of the city which are applied. The only demands made on the local community are for its land and labour.

Integrated and catalytic development

Building on some of the ideas expressed in these studies, this writer (Pearce, 1978a) has proposed a more general two-fold classification based on the division of responsibility in the development process:

1. 'Integrated' development implies development by a single promoter or developer to the exclusion of all other participation.
2. 'Catalytic' development, on the contrary, occurs when the initial activities of a major developer generate complementary developments by other companies or individuals.

This basic difference in the division of responsibility influences not only the nature of the development process but also the form of the resulting resort, its location and, to a certain degree, the type of clientele served.

Integrated development

The concept of the 'integrated' ski resort (Cumin, 1970) is now generally accepted in France where La Plagne remains the classic example. Other resorts exhibiting similar characteristics to La Plagne have developed independently elsewhere – for example, the new marinas along the Mediterranean coastline – and it is possible to enlarge on Cumin's

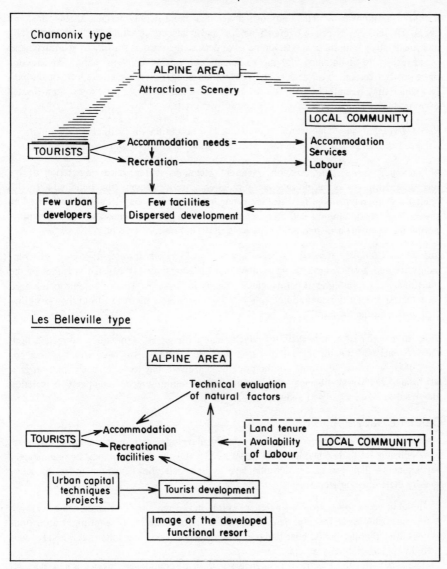

2.3 Préau's scenarios of alpine tourist development.
(After Préau, 1970)

ideas and extend these to embrace a more general process of development characterized by the factors described below.

A single promoter.   The entire resort is developed by a single promoter or company. This one company must have at its disposal adequate financial and technical resources. Consequently, such developments are generally limited to large metropolitan financial concerns. Local participation is thus largely excluded from the development process although some locals may find work in the construction and subsequent staffing of the resort and local authorities may be induced to undertake public works programmes such as roading.

Balanced development.   This unity of management more readily permits, though does not necessarily ensure, effective overall planning and balanced development, both technically and financially. With but a single source of direction, the ratio of ski-lifts to apartments can more readily be maintained and the technical problems inherent in marina construction more easily overcome (Giraud, 1971). A common budget allows those aspects of the project which may be initially unprofitable (e.g. the installation of ski-lifts) to be compensated by more lucrative operations (e.g. the sale of real estate).

Rapid development.   This technical and financial co-ordination facilitates very rapid, yet balanced, development which in turn permits a short-term return on the capital invested.

A functional form.   Co-ordination, coherent planning, and physical integration of the resort's facilities may result in a very functional form whereby the holidaymaker, his habitat and his recreational facilities are brought together in a very localized and close-knit resort. Thus condominiums and hotels cluster at the very foot of the ski slopes and marinas permit the yachtsman to step out of his back door and on to his yacht.

Isolation.   Complete freedom is necessary to develop such resorts, thus they are commonly located away from existing settlements, on comparatively isolated stretches of the coastline or above the line of permanent settlement in the Alps. This complements the need for integration with the natural elements but further removes the resort from the possibility of insertion in the local milieu.

High status.   The first-rate facilities which such a functional resort offers attracts a high class of tourists. Thus the increased costs which are normally associated with the development of isolated sites (even though the price of land itself may be less) are offset by higher tariffs and the overall financial structure of the operation. Indeed, comparative isolation may even enhance the resort's status.

Catalytic development

Elsewhere a single promoter may dominate the development process without, however, monopolising it. Rather his activities serve as a 'catalyst' by stimulating complementary developments. This process, which might be termed 'catalytic' development, is characterized by the following steps:

1. Initial impetus comes from a single large promoter, often a major outside company, who provides the basic facilities and the conditions for 'take-off'; the primary attractions (ski-lifts, thermal baths, boat harbour), major accommodation units (large hotels, condominiums), publicity and promotion.
2. The success of these activities engenders a spirit of confidence, creates a new demand and encourages the development of complementary facilities: secondary recreational facilities (night clubs, bars, cinemas, bus excursions, mini-golf, etc), alternative accommodation (chalets, small hotels, *pensions*, furnished rooms) and shops. These projects require more modest investments, thus permitting the active participation of smaller local companies and individuals in the development and management of the resort.
3. The expansion of the resort now depends essentially on the operation of a free market system with both the principal promoter and the secondary developers providing facilities to meet the demand. However, if these secondary developers do not respond sufficiently then the principal promoter will have to step up his own activities in order to safeguard the profitability of his existing operations. Conversely, it is also essential to guard against excessive speculation and over-development. In some cases the principal

promoter may impose a predetermined programme on the secondary developers, in others planning regulations or the judicious intervention of the local authority may effectively control growth.

The resulting resort differs significantly from the integrated one. Firstly, catalytic developments are usually grafted on to existing settlements. There, however, the major projects often locate some distance away from the centre around which are concentrated the activities of the locals on their existing property. Secondly, the presence of existing dwellings, together with the multiplicity of developers and the less intensive nature of their projects, gives rise to a much more diverse and less concentrated resort than that which results from integrated development. The range of accommodation types offered also broadens the base of the resort which may attract several different classes of visitor.

Five French examples have been selected to illustrate in more detail the characteristics of these two processes. The 'integrated' examples include a ski complex (La Grande Plagne) and two marinas (Port Grimaud and the Marines de Cogolin), while the 'catalytic' process is illustrated by a ski resort (Vars) and a spa (Gréoux-les-Bains).

La Grande Plagne

The development of the Bellecote–Montjovet massif in Savoy, France, into the tourist complex known today as La Grande Plagne began in the early 1960s. Faced with declining agricultural returns and the closure of local lead mines, five communes in the Isere valley joined together in a 'syndicat intercommunal' to promote the development of their mountain resources. Although the communes built an access road to the chosen high altitude site (at 2,000 m), the first developer, a modest regional company, soon failed financially. Subsequently a group of banks, mainly based in Paris, established a development company, the SAP (Société d'Aménagement de La Plagne), and entered into a formal contract with the communes in December 1961. Basically this contract specified that the SAP would have the exclusive rights to construct a network of lifts and accompanying accommodation at a predetermined rate while the communes would concede the land occupied by the ski-field for thirty years for a small percentage of the lift revenue and would make available for sale the land on which the resort would be built.

Construction of La Plagne, the base resort, began the following year. Several levels of integration can be seen in the development of La Plagne, widely acknowledged as the first 'integrated' resort. Firstly, La Plagne was developed entirely by the SAP. By 1968 the company had built 5,000 beds, mainly in condominiums, with a lift network having an hourly capacity of 9,000 skiers. While the operation of the lifts was initially unprofitable, the sale of apartments, block by block, assured a rapid return on capital invested, permitting the self-financing of the whole operation. The SAP also managed or subsidized certain shops and hotels as well as the cinema during these first years as their presence was essential to attract would-be buyers. However, it is in the form of the resort that integration is the most evident. All the accommodation is located at 2,000 m, high above the traditional settlements situated in the valley below, on a small shelf towards which converge the principal pistes and from which leave the major lifts (Fig. 2.4). Moreover, the amount of accommodation has been calculated as a function of the capacity of the ski-field to ensure that the benefits of this functional association are not marred by over-crowding of the slopes. There is also a virtual physical integration of the thirty or so buildings that constitute La Plagne. Use of motor vehicles within La Plagne is consequently much reduced while those vehicles arriving at the north side of the resort are effectively separated by its linear form from the skiers on the south side. This integration also limits the amount of land to be purchased, reduces servicing costs, enables a more rational use of central heating and permits easier maintenance and management.

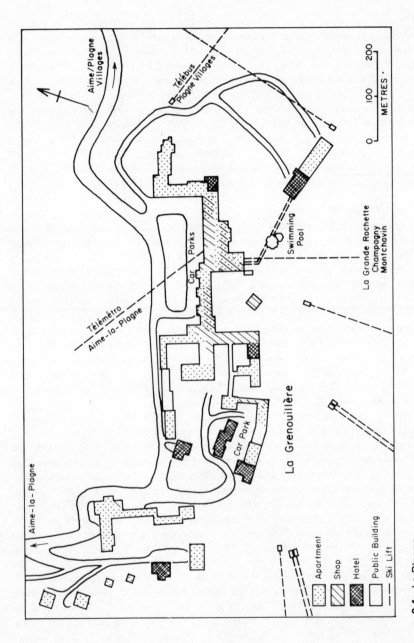

Aime/Plagne
Villages

Télébus
Plagne Villages

Télémétro
Aime-la-Plagne

Car Parks

Aime-la-Plagne

Car Park

La Grenouillère

Swimming
Pool

La Grande Rochette
Champagny
Montchavin

0 100 200
METRES ·

Apartment
Shop
Hotel
Public Building
Ski Lift

2.4 La Plagne.

With La Plagne established, the SAP progressively developed four smaller satellite resorts nearby at a comparable altitude. In one of these, Aime La Plagne (or Aime 2000), integration is carried to the extreme as a single gigantic monolith accommodates not only 2,500 people but also houses a cinema, discotheque, restaurant and a full range of shops. However, there is a move away from this total integration in the subsequent satellites such as Plagne Villages. This reflects changing market demands although the clientele for these satellites continues to be drawn from the same professional classes as for La Plagne itself, particularly from the 'Polytechniciens' from Paris.

Other than employment in some of the new jobs created, the local population has been effectively excluded from the development of La Plagne and the other high altitude satellite resorts. However, the opening up of the immense ski-field by the SAP has enabled the communes to undertake more traditional developments (small hotels, chalets, holiday camps, gîtes) around existing settlements further down the mountain (Longefoy, 1,550 m; Montchavin, 1,300 m; Champagny 1,250 m). These are joined to the upper ski basins by a series of linking lifts and are being developed as part of the overall complex of La Grande Plagne.

In this broader context the high altitude integrated resorts may be thought of as having had a catalytic effect on the area as a whole. The question of scale is therefore very important in assessing tourist development. By 1974 La Grande Plagne had an accommodation capacity of 14,000 beds, forty-five lifts and eighty ski trails totalling 135 km. An estimated 500,000 skiers visited the complex during the 1973–74 season.

Port Grimaud and the Marines de Cogolin

Parallels to La Plagne are to be found in some of the new coastal developments where boating replaces skiing and where the resort is orientated around a boat harbour or mooring berths rather than in relation to the pistes. Two neighbouring resorts on the Gulf of St Tropez, Port Grimaud and the Marines de Cogolin, provide a different spatial expression of a common principle, the integration of the vacationer into his recreational environment (Fig. 5.5). Each resort is the work of a single external developer. Port Grimaud was developed by an Alsatian architect and the Marines de Cogolin by the Paris-based Navi-Service. Moreover, Navi-Service's intervention followed the failure of a small regional venture. Technical and financial aspects of marina development, such as the need to closely co-ordinate the construction of the port or berths with the housing programme, favours such unity of development, but the failure of the local population to have initiated any coastal developments has an underlying geographical explanation. The main settlement in each commune, respectively Grimaud and Cogolin, is located some kilometres inland where the major activities are centred on viticulture and the manufacture of pipes. The local residents did not have a maritime outlook, as at nearby St Tropez. Furthermore, the marshy land subsequently developed was considered virtually worthless and attracted little local interest. The municipalities have done little more than grant the building permits. A few Grimaudois and Cogolinois have found new jobs in the resorts, but among the new shopkeepers several Tropezians represent the only local initiative.

Vars

The catalytic effect of the intervention of a large outside company is clearly evident at Vars (Hautes Alpes). Although the commune's potential as a major ski resort was recognized before the Second World War, the few hundred Varsins, for the most part small farmers, lacked the means to develop more than four or five simple tows and a few small hotels and chalets in the immediate post-war period. With local agriculture in decline, the commune was stagnating and suffering steady population losses through out-migration. This situation changed in 1958, with the election of a new mayor, a former politician from Paris. The new mayor was able to interest a group of Paris-based financial concerns in forming a company, the (Société pour l'Equipement et le Développement de Vars) SEDEV, to develop Vars as a tourist resort. Unlike the local population, the SEDEV had both the financial and technical resources to create a network of lifts large enough to launch the resort on a national scale. As the SEDEV constructs each stage of the network the commune, in the terms of a formal contract, cedes a specified area of land to the company for the development of accommodation. The SEDEV has limited itself to large-scale condominium development, leaving open the possibility of alternative forms of accommodation. Previously reluctant to take the initiative, the Varsins responded enthusiastically to the signing of the agreement with the SEDEV in 1962. From this date the register of building permits shows a marked increase in local activity; new chalets are built, small hotels and pensions are opened or enlarged, a shop-window is improved here, a new shop built there, snack bars and 'boites de nuit' appear. Most of this activity, assisted by loans from government agencies such as the Crédit Hotelier and the Crédit Agricole, has been concentrated around the existing hamlets (Ste Catherine, Ste Marie and St Marcellin) while the SEDEV and other non-local companies have developed a new centre at Les Claux (69 per cent of tourist beds in 1972), some 3 km up the valley. The municipality was responsible for purchasing the necessary land at Les Claux and for servicing and subdividing it. Other new secondary roads were also built, together with an improved sewerage system. The municipality also entered directly into the tourist industry with the construction of accommodation in the form of 'gites', hostels and apartments. Throughout, it has had to rely on extensive loans from central government.

By 1972, ten years after the contract with the SEDEV had been signed, Vars had an accommodation capacity of more than 8,600 beds and a network of twenty-five lifts. Much of the resort's success has clearly been due to the strong and able character of the mayor who has been able to balance local interests with those of the external developers and control the rate of growth through the judicous granting of building permits and the application of the municipal building code.

Gréoux-les-Bains

Over the same period an identical process led to the expansion of Gréoux-les-Bains, a spa in the Alpes de Haute Provence. Its small, family-run thermal establishment steadily deteriorating for want of capital, Gréoux-les-Bains was faced with stagnation until the sale in 1962 of the baths to the Compagnie Française du Thermalisme, the largest private thermal group in France. The new company launched a two-fold development programme; the renovation, modernization and expansion of the baths was accompanied by the construction of hotels and apartments to meet the new demand. These were located in close proximity to the baths, a kilometre or so from the town centre. However, after assuring a certain amount of new accommodation the company concentrated on the expansion of the baths (whose operation is profitable in itself). Subsequent demand was taken up by the local residents, the Grysliens. Several of the older hotels were renovated and enlarged and three new ones were built. There was also a noticeable expansion in the number of rooms let and an upgrading of the facilities in these. Not only are furnished rooms a popular form of accommodation in today's spa towns but they also do not necessitate large investments and require little entrepreneurial skill. A number of new shops have also appeared and a variety of bus excursions are now offered. Other Grysliens find employment as baths attendants. Once again the effect of outside intervention and stimulus has been most marked. Gréoux-les-Bains received 11,200 'curistes' in 1973 compared to only 2,500 a decade earlier. While much of the profit from the baths has flowed back to Paris there can be little doubt that the community as a whole has greatly benefited from this increase.

Core–periphery development

Throughout these typologies certain core–periphery relationships emerge. In each case there is a class of development characterized by the dominance of external, usually metropolitan-based, developers who have the financial, technical and commercial capacity to develop peripheral tourist resources, frequently on a very large scale. In many cases the resorts created by urban promoters also serve a predominantly urban clientele so that metropolitan dominance of the development process is complete. This core-periphery relationship is most explicit in Préau's Les Belleville scenario but is also inherent in Barbaza's Black Sea class, the 'rapid growth' category of Peck and Lepie and the 'integrated' resorts described by Pearce.

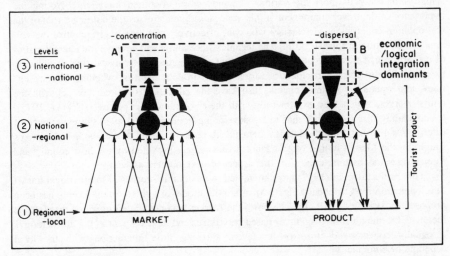

EXPLANATORY NOTE

Two separate structures, A and B link up through a bulk-carrying transport function, forming the functional mechanism. Each structure has **three levels** of operations, which partake in the **basic processes** – concentration and dispersal. In structure A the lowest functional level is regional-local, representing the market areas, from where potential tourist consumers are activated by level II marketing functions (travel bureaus, tour operators, travel clubs, etc.). The next upward movement, to level III, illustrates the bulking in preparation for the ultimate A-to-B geographic transfer. The dispersal process involves a structured descent within the tourist product, via the arrival mechanism (level III) to the resort-accommodation facilities (level II) where the dispersal tends to stabilize. The usually insignificant interaction with the local level, economic as well as cultural, is indicated by reciprocal arrows.

Horizontal interaction occurs on level II, and obviously on level III. For structure A this demonstrates the complementary role of operating service agents. In B the level II interaction illustrates an enclavic, institutionalized tourist circulation between resort facilities, a process often actively promoted by hotel management, or a certain type of resort hotel. This accentuated circulation within the level is at the expense of further direct dispersal of the tourist flow to the indigenous local level.

Horizontal and vertical economic/logistical integration dominants (dotted lines), link together structures, levels, and associated functions. Greytone symbols illustrate a wholly integrated system in terms of financing, management control, organization and dimensioning. International airlines – British Airways, Pan Am and T.W.A. – institutional industrial conglomerates, sometimes with vested interests in transportation – I.T.T., oil companies – typify the integrated sector of the mechanism.

2.5 Hills and Lundgren's core–periphery model.
    (Hills and Lundgren, 1977)

However, it is at the international scale that the core–periphery nature of certain tourist development is the most evident. At this scale, the wealthier urban industrial nations constitute the core or generating areas for less developed peripheral countries which become tourist destinations. Examples of this relationship include Western Europe – the Mediterranean, North America – the Caribbean and Australia and New Zealand – the South Pacific. Turner and Ash (1975) have coined the term 'pleasure periphery' while Lundgren (1972) describes these relationships as: 'a metropolitan economic hegemony par excellence'.

According to Lundgren (1972, pp. 86–7), these relationships: 'are basically a function of the technological and economic superiority of the travel-generating, metropolitan core areas as such and the willingness of the destination areas to adopt metropolitan values and solutions in order to meet the various demands of metropolitan travellers'. Noting the importance of the travel component at this scale, Lundgren stresses the dominant role of the metropolitan countries as air carriers who can, effectively and selectively, control the volume and direction of tourist traffic. The technical, economic and commercial characteristics of modern tourist travel favour the development of integrated enterprises, further reducing the possibility of local participation. Moreover, metropolitan firms, whether they are airlines, tour operators or hotel chains, also have the advantage of direct contact with the tourist market, which they exploit fully with their commercial expertise (IUOTO, 1975). Compounding this is the fact that many developing countries lack even the experience of catering for a strong domestic tourism demand. As a result, many of the goods and services sought by the foreign tourist often cannot be adequately provided by the host country and foreign operators assume control of this aspect of development as well.

Hills and Lundgren (1977) have attempted to model this process of international tourist development in the Caribbean (Fig. 2.5). A similar model of tourism in the Pacific has been proposed by Britton (1980). In each case, the market is concentrated upwards through the hierarchy by integrated metropolitan-based enterprises and development in the destination is essentially concentrated in resort enclaves, allowing little interaction with the local economy or community.

It must be remembered, however, that these are models of international tourist development in Third World countries and that most international tourist traffic is between developed countries in Western Europe and North America. Here the host country itself usually has the capacity to cater for much of the foreign tourist demand and the pattern of development and ownership would be quite different from that of the Caribbean or the Pacific (Collins, 1977). Unfortunately no attempt has yet been made to derive a more general classification of international tourist development.

Conclusions

This chapter has attempted to provide a basis for examining tourist development. First the various sectors of supply were introduced and the roles of different development agents were discussed before a range of typologies of tourist development were reviewed. These typologies by no means exhaust the possible ways in which tourism has evolved at different times and in different places. Tourism based on second homes, for example, is commonly characterized by the multiplicity of developers involved, each acquiring or building his own particular property. However, the different criteria employed in these typologies, together with the earlier structured examination of sectors and agents, provides a framework for analysing tourism in other situations to see how it has developed to date or how it may evolve in the future.

CHAPTER 3
EVALUATING TOURIST RESOURCES

Tourism, like other economic and social activities, does not occur evenly or randomly in space. Certain sites, locations or regions are more favourable for tourist development than others. One avenue of geographic enquiry is to examine and explain existing patterns of tourist development in terms of a range of locational attributes. Applied geographers, however, may be more interested in identifying potential sites or regions for development, though the examination of existing patterns may form an important part of this process. The problem may be assessing the feasibility of developing a particular site, the selection of one site from a number of alternatives for a specific project or the broader evaluation of an area in terms of general tourist potential. The place of such evaluation in the overall planning process is examined more fully in Chapter 5. The present chapter discusses first of all the various locational factors which influence tourist development and how these may be assessed. These individual factors are then brought together in a general review of techniques and methodologies for evaluating tourist resources. The chapter concludes with a short case study which examines the relative importance and interaction of the locational factors related to a specific form of development, namely ski-fields.

LOCATIONAL FACTORS

The factors influencing the location of tourist projects or the tourist potential of an area can be grouped into seven broad categories – climate, physical conditions, attractions, access, land tenure and use, constraints and incentives and 'other' factors (e.g. labour costs, political stability). These factors are inter-related and the categories are not wholly exclusive. Climate, for example, may be an attraction; the attractiveness of an area may depend in part on its access and certain forms of land tenure may be subject to various constraints. Nevertheless, the categories outlined do provide an appropriate focus for the literature reviewed as well as a useful introduction to the methodologies discussed subsequently. The importance of any one of these factors will depend on the type of development and especially on the scale of analysis. Climatic data, for example, may suggest broad regions which may be suitable for developing tourism, but within a resort in any one of these accessibility will be a prime determinant for the successful location of a specific hotel or motel. The selection of an area or the scale of development proposed will also depend on the extent to which the area may be developed. Studies of carrying capacity may thus form an integral part of the evaluation process. Such studies are reviewed at the conclusion of this first section.

Climate

Although the relationships between tourism and climate have long been recognized, comparatively little research has been directed specifically at the nature of these relationships (Mings, 1978a). Climatic variations affect tourist development in a number of ways:

Attraction

A favourable climate can be one of the major attractions of an area, as testified by the popularity of Mediterranean, Caribbean and Pacific destinations. It is simply pleasant and agreeable to spend one's holidays in an area characterized by warm temperatures and high sunshine hours. This 'hunt for the sun', however, is a comparatively recent phenomenon. Although the mildness of the winter climate of the Riviera has been appreciated since the eighteenth century, it was considered unhealthy to remain on the coast into July and August and it is not until the mid 1930s that the summer visitors surpassed the 'hivernants'. This example serves well to emphasize at the outset that resources are, after all, cultural appraisals. Other resorts owe, or owed, their popularity to mild or invigorating climates, such as the hill stations of India and the Far East (Robinson, 1972; Senftleben, 1973) and Europe's 'stations climatiques' like Leysin and Superbagnères. More specific forms of tourism, such as that based on winter sports, will depend heavily on other climatic criteria. For other forms still, such as sightseeing or cultural tourism, a favourable climate may be an important secondary factor. Conversely, adverse climatic conditions will detract from an area's interest or beauty and the absence of certain conditions, for example snow, will prohibit certain activities altogether.

Seasonality

Favourable climatic conditions for any specific activity will often occur only during certain seasons. The degree of seasonality will have a marked bearing on an area's profitability. Longer seasons give a better utilization of plant and equipment and consequently yield higher returns on capital invested. Blessed are those regions with a 'second season'. Seasonality will become more important as the dependence on climatic factors increases. The length of season will be more critical for coastal and winter sports resorts than for capital city tourism. In India, Singh (1975, p. 42) notes that: 'the odyssean spirit of wanderlust seems to be overcoming the climatic barriers'. There is little variation in tourist arrivals from one season to another and religion based tourism appears wholly independent of climatic comforts. Singh also notes how the richer tourists can afford air-conditioning and other amenities reducing the influence of adverse climatic conditions.

Construction

Development costs will rise where the construction period is limited by seasonal climatic constraints such as rainy seasons or harsh winters. Additional costs will also be incurred where extreme temperatures increase the need for central heating or air conditioning (Mings, 1978a). In the case of La Plagne (Fig. 2.4), the physical integration of the resort is in part a response to the practicalities of heating buildings located at 2,000 m and the functional form of the apartments is a reflection of the shortened construction season. Micro-climatic considerations are also important in the design of coastal resorts; for example, siting swimming pools so that they are not constantly in the shadow of high rise hotels.

Operations

Short period climatic events may hinder the operation of certain facilities. High winds may lead to the closure of aerial cableways and severe storms will limit yachting or sightseeing cruises and may disrupt access. Strong coastal breezes may give rise to unpleasant conditions on sandy beaches and recurrent ground fogs will restrict aircraft operations. The length of activity-day may be severely limited in harsh winter regimes.

The geographical problem here is to identify those areas or regions within a given study area which are climatically suitable for some form of tourist development or recreational activity. Several attempts have been made to derive recreational climatic classifications through grouping a number of elements deemed to affect recreational activity and tourist comfort.

In his classification of the Canadian North-West Territories, Crowe (1975) selected three factors for each of the two main seasons (*winter* – length of activity-day, temperature, wind; *summer* – temperature, cloud cover, wind) and defined for each limiting values for 'ideal', 'marginal' and 'sub-marginal' classes. These factor classes were then combined to give four classes of outdoor activity potential, with each factor given equal weighting. A similar approach was adopted by Day *et al*. (1977), to map variations in suitability for winter sports and summer activities in Bay of Fundy National Park. Four parameters were used for classifying areas of climatic suitability for skiing and snow-mobiling – temperature, wind speed, precipitation and visibility. Areas described as most suitable meet all four criteria, those described as climatically least suitable meet one or none (Fig. 3.1).

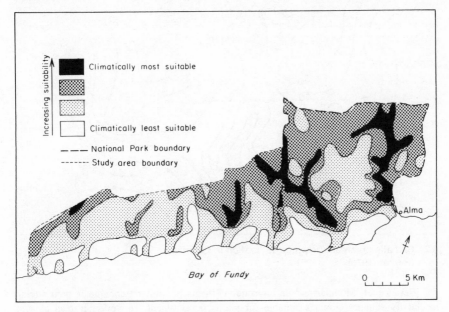

3.1 Climatic zones related to snowmobiling and skiing, January, Bay of Fundy. (Day *et al*., 1977)

Where more adequate data are available, a more quantitative approach can be adopted. In his recreational climatic study of Ontario, Crowe (1975) considered two main factors – comfort and weather – for a range of summer activities – landscape touring, vigorous activity and 'beaching'. Comfort was expressed in terms of maximum temperature and humidity and weather in terms of cloud cover and precipitation. Percentiles were then calculated for each factor and combined into a general index for each activity. The results of the summer analysis indicated that conditions for beaching were much better in

Southern Ontario and that other parts of the province were more favourable for landscape touring and vigorous activities.

A different approach was used by Harker (1973) in her classification of the climatic potential of the whole of Canada for winter recreation. Seven factors were selected and the values for each given different weightings (e.g. mean annual total snowfall was considered more important than humidity). The weighted scores for each of the seven factors were then summed for fifty points throughout Canada, and mapped to give an isopleth map showing the climatic suitability of different parts of the country for establishing winter sports (Fig. 3.2). A general correspondence was found between the areas identified as having a high potential and those where ski resorts were already well established.

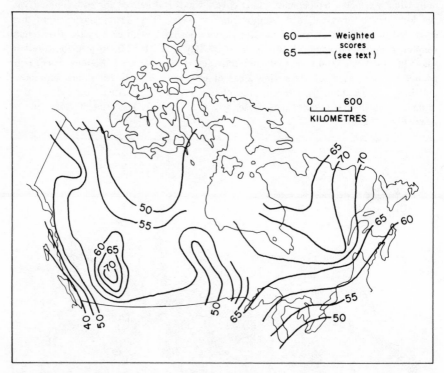

3.2 Climatic potential for winter recreation in Canada.
(Harker, 1973)

Besancenot, Mounier and de Lavenne (1978) use a similar technique in their attempt to classify summer climates suitable for tourist development. However, instead of summing the values of the six parameters used, a range of values is defined for each parameter to give a ninefold classification. The parameters used – sunshine hours, cloud cover, maximum temperature, wind speed, vapour pressure and precipitation – are said to combine a measure of comfort with one of attractivity. These writers also reject the use of average values, such as monthly means, in favour of actual daily recorded values, as they argue it is these which are the most meaningful for the tourist. This information is then presented in histograms for ten-day periods for a number of Breton and Mediterranean resorts. However, when it comes to mapping summer conditions at a regional level this is done simply in terms of the number of fine days per month.

Besancenot *et al.* also stress that tourists are concerned with how reliable or variable resort climates are. Climatic variability was measured by the use of the coefficient of variation, values for which were shown to decline over the summer months with latitude. Moreover, variability diminishes where climatic conditions are the most favourable. However, Dauphiné and Ghilardi's (1978) review of climatic comfort indices with reference to the Côte d'Azur shows that the extent of seasonal variability depends in part on the index used. Clausse's index shows little variability in summer but much in winter whereas the converse is true of Terjung's.

A further recreational comfort index is proposed by Yapp and McDonald (1978), using a model of the heat balance of the human body and based on the maximum use of actual observations and minimum use of average values. As the human heat balance depends in part on the activity level, the model was applied to different recreational activities such as sunbathing, walking and boat fishing and the frequency of conditions that are pleasant, indifferent or unsuitable for these was calculated.

Although as yet far from perfect these attempts to define tourist climates suggest that it is insufficient merely to consider a single element, such as temperature, or a series of elements, as has often been the case in the past. Some attempt must be made to combine particular parameters into a more general index and one which is related specifically to particular recreational or tourist activities. The measures discussed here show it is possible to identify spatial and temporal variations in such indices. In this last respect it is important to note that periods identified by several writers as being climatically suitable for tourism were significantly longer than the periods of actual tourist use.

Physical conditions

Physical conditions, other than climatic ones, are important in several aspects of tourist development, particularly at the resort level.

Building site

Firstly, there must be a sufficiently large site to locate the required accommodation, supporting facilities and necessary infrastructure. Soils, geology, topography, slope stability and aspect will be among the many physical site attributes to be considered. Additional factors will include the possibilities for water supply, drainage and sewage disposal.

Access

Ease of access, as determined by these attributes, will also be important, particularly for winter sports resorts and development based on natural attractions. Modern technology can overcome access to most sites as indeed it can enable construction in most places. The costs involved, however, may be prohibitive.

Recreational resources

The recreational base of many resorts depends on their physical attributes. Georgulas (1970), for instance, proposes the following criteria for a first-class beach:

1. *For passive activities* – a combination of the following: (a) Beaches – fine clean sand, 300 feet minimum length and 50 feet minimum width. Beach should be relatively free of exposure for at least 80 per cent of the year. (b) Backland – shade, tree, hospitable environment, free from man-made nuisances (e.g. dumping) and natural nuisances (e.g. poisonous insects, snakes). Slope less than 15° for easy access and potential for development.

2. *For active activities* – Water quality: No (or very little) silting, colour – less than 5 Hazen units, odourless, coliform count less than 50 per 100 ml, free of biological nuisances, sea-bed free of coral and sharp rocks to 8 feet depth during high tide, free of dangerous currents. The beach and immediate water area should have a gradient of not more than 8°. Beach quality as in (1) but longer and wider. Swimming should be possible for nine months of year.

Ski-field development will of course depend on other physical criteria (see below) as will the construction of marinas. More generally, other physical features are major attractions in themselves; for example, the Grand Canyon in Colorado, Franz Josef Glacier in New Zealand and the Iguazu Falls along the Brazil/Argentine border. Classification of attractions constitutes a problem in itself.

Attractions

'Tourist development is a problem of matching naturally or historically given resources to the demands and preferences of actual or potential tourists' (Piperoglou, 1967, p. 169). However, as Guthrie (1961) has pointed out, the motivations for foreign travel are extremely diverse and there is no universal measure of tourist attractiveness. Different people will view different phenomena in different ways. Ritter (1975) for example, comments on the 'neglect of the seacoast' in Lebanon and throughout the Islamic world. Moreover, as we have seen earlier, there is a wide range of phenomena which may attract tourists. For the purposes of spatial differentiation, the task facing the geographer or planner is: 'to reduce phenomena of aesthetic or cultural significance to quantifiable magnitudes for purposes of comparative evaluation' (Piperoglou, 1967, p. 169).

Piperoglou outlines four basic steps in evaluating tourist attractions:

1. Survey the market to discover tourist preferences.
2. Identify and evaluate what tourists want in the area of study.
3. Define regions in terms of the spatial interplay of resources.
4. Check the capacity of the study region to absorb visitors in terms of both the human and space factor.

The first three of these will be dealt with here, the fourth being considered in the section on carrying capacity.

Thus for his study of western Greece, Piperoglou undertook a survey of visitors to Greece. Three main groups of attractions were identified: 'Ancient Greece', 'picturesque villages' and 'sun and sea'. Resources in the study area were then evaluated and plotted on a series of overlay maps, each resource being represented by a circle proportional to the preferences expressed in the survey. In evaluating particular resources, attention was paid to the extent to which it was unique or occurred elsewhere in Greece. Tourist regions were then defined on the basis of the coincidence of different resources within a given area, in this case within an 80 km radius of a base point. Such a distance was considered the average a tourist would willingly travel on a half day trip to a point of interest. Where two of the three main resources were present, the circles were expanded to their square and to the third power when all were evident. A fourth weighted element, an infrastructural component in the form of an urban settlement of 50,000 people or more, was also introduced. Scores for each region were then summed and development priorities determined on the basis of the total score of each region. This approach then combines the weighting of various attractions with the spatial association of these. The clustering of resources is especially important, the whole being greater than the sum of the individual attractions, especially where a range of different resources occurs.

Table 3.1 Relative importance of socio-cultural elements influencing the cultural attractiveness of a tourist region. (Ritchie and Zins, 1978)

FACTOR	ORDINAL RANK OF IMPORTANCE		AVERAGE IMPORTANCE ON INTERVAL SCALE		INTERVAL ORDER OF IMPORTANCE		OVERALL ORDER OF IMPORTANCE	
	R	N-R	R	N-R	R	N-R	R	N-R
Leisure activities	1	1	9.18	8.54	1	2	1	1
Gastronomy	2	3	8.63	8.32	2	1	2	2
Handicrafts	3	2	7.95	8.66	4	3	3	3
Traditions	4	4	8.34	7.80	3	5	3	4
History	5	5	7.65	8.24	6	4	5	4
Art/Music	6	6	7.66	7.38	5	6	5	6
Architecture	7	7	7.01	7.22	7	7	7	7
Work	8	8	6.19	6.88	8	8	8	8
Language	9	9	5.55	5.64	9	9	9	9
Education	10	10	4.77	4.87	10	10	10	10
Dress	11	11	3.73	4.56	12	11	11	11
Religion	12	12	4.02	3.87	11	12	11	12

R = Residents
N-R = Non residents

Visitor surveys can be costly in terms of both time and money. A second technique is to survey expert opinion, commonly using the Delphi method, as a surrogate for tourist preferences. In seeking to establish the importance of culture as a determinant of tourist attractiveness, Ritchie and Zins (1978) contacted some 200 'informed individuals'. Respondents were asked by questionnaire to consider a range of factors from the stand-point of an 'average traveller'. Responses were then measured both on ordinal rank scales and on eleven point interval scales. In general terms, cultural and social characteristics were found to rank second behind natural beauty and climate but ahead of other factors such as accessibility and attitudes towards tourists. The relative importance of the different socio-cultural elements was then determined for residents and non-residents (Table 3.1). Unfortunately, in this article this first stage was not related to the actual evaluation of resources in a specific region.

In his comprehensive survey of tourist resources in Southern Africa, Ferrario (1979) combines features of each of these methodologies. Firstly, 2,300 different features mentioned in ten guidebooks on South Africa were inventoried and classified into 21 categories. These were then evaluated in terms of two criteria – appeal and availability, using the formula $I = \dfrac{A + B}{2}$ – where I is the index of tourist potential, A is the appeal component, or demand, B is the availability component, or supply.

Demand was first assessed by a large scale visitor survey. A strong preference was shown amongst the twenty-one categories listed for environmental features, namely scenery and landscape, wildlife and natural vegetation. The percentage of preference received for each category was taken as an index of tourist demand and reduced to a scale of from 1 to 10 (e.g. 77 per cent became an index of 7.7). Each of the 2,300 individual attractions in Southern Africa was then evaluated by weighting its category index by a guidebook coefficient, that is by how many of the ten guidebooks reported it. To bring back the resulting value to a 1 to 10 scale, the square root of the product was taken. With the inclusion of this new weighting coefficient (G), the formula thus became $I = \dfrac{\sqrt{AG + B}}{2}$

The B values or the index of accessibility were determined by the use of six criteria said to affect supply: seasonality, accessibility, admission, importance, fragility and popularity. 'Community influentials' throughout the country were then asked to rank individual attractions in their area in terms of these six criteria according to a descriptive nominal scale. These responses were subsequently transformed into a weighted numerical index and the different evaluations received by each attraction were then averaged. After plotting these values, clusters of attractions were identified for grid cells and further weighted by attendance figures on the principle that the sum of many low indices in a grid cell representing a cluster of less important features, could not be numerically equivalent to the presence in another cell of a single high index of a leading attraction. Finally, twenty tourist regions were identified in the combined territory of South Africa, Lesotho and Swaziland by the clustering of grid cells. These were found to correspond well with existing patterns of demand, though this is perhaps not surprising given the final heavy weighting by attendance figures.

Although not without their limitations, these papers do suggest that it is possible to evaluate reasonably objectively such an abstract and intangible concept as attractivity and to delimit spatial variations in its occurrence.

Access

Two associated types of access are important in assessing potential locations for tourist development: physical access and market access.

Physical access will depend to a large degree on the existing infrastructure – the location of access routes, highways and railways, the proximity of airports. As such infrastructure is costly to provide, its presence or absence is very significant. The extent to which timetables and route schedules service destinations already equipped is also critical. As the development of aircraft technology has enabled the growth of longer and longer direct flights, some localities, especially island destinations, are now being 'over-flown' in the same way that many small localities previously served by rail are now bypassed. Relative isolation will only be an advantage where the emphasis is on a luxury market and the exclusion of mass tourism.

Accessibility is also a feature of proximity to the market, whether measured in terms of travel time, cost or distance. At the international level, proximity to industrialized and urbanized countries with high standards of living will be important. The nearness of large urban areas and the characteristics of their populations (age, income) will be deciding factors at the national and regional level. Different types of development will demand differing degrees of market access. Many second homes are used not only during long vacations but also at weekends. Proximity to the primary residence is therefore important and the majority of second homes appear to be within 100–150 miles (160–240 km) of major population centres. However, distances vary from country to country, being greater in the United States and smaller in Sweden (Coppock, 1977). For more specialized attractions, such as ski-fields and outstanding natural features, tourists will be prepared to travel greater distances. For developments which do not constitute a tourist ensemble in themselves, proximity to the market becomes particularly critical. Such is the case with the location of pleasure ports, the demand for berths depending on the resident population and the number of second homes in a region. In the Var (France), the ratio is approximately one berth for boats greater than two tons for every ten second homes (Perret and Bruère, 1970).

Much work on predicting flows to particular resorts and developments has centred on the use of gravity models (Archer and Shea, 1973). The basic gravity model expressed the flow of people between two centres as a function of the population of each and the distance between them according to the formula $I = \dfrac{P1P2}{d}$, where I = interaction, $P1$ = the population of one of the places, $P2$ = population of the other place, and d = distance between. Tourist flows, however, are not necessarily reciprocal as Wolfe (1970) points out in the case of second homes where the traffic outward from an urban area to a cottage resort is not complemented by a reverse flow to the city. Consequently, when applied to tourist flows, the basic gravity model has been modified in various ways. Such modifications include the incorporation of variables measuring the attractiveness of the destinations (the number of ski-lifts, the ratio of water to land area) or the measurement of distance in terms of time or travel cost. Modified gravity models have been applied with some success to specific cases such as the demand for second homes and ski-fields (Bell, 1977; McAllister and Klett, 1976) and to tourist travel to Las Vegas (Malamud, 1973).

In many cases, it will be not so much actual distances which will determine an area's potential market as its location relative to other resorts or attractions. Several major projects have been developed as 'intervening opportunities', exploiting their location between existing resorts and the market. Developers of the Languedoc-Roussillon littoral, for example, sought in part to intercept holidaymakers heading for Spain. Cancun in Mexico has been promoted as a Caribbean destination, and one which is closer to many United States cities than more traditional resorts in Jamaica or Puerto Rico (Collins, 1979).

Land tenure and use

The purchase of land or the acquisition of rights to occupy a site is a necessary prerequisite for any tourist development project. The spontaneous development of second homes usually involves a series of individual initiatives on the part of both the buyers and sellers. Consequently, small plots of land are common in this type of development. In the case of large, planned projects and the creation 'ex-nihilo' of resorts, speedy acquisition of extensive tracts of land at the outset of the operation is important. Access to the required land gives the freedom to develop the resort as a whole, to construct it as an integral and functional unit according to specific architectural or town-planning principles. Rapid acquisition of the land is likely to minimize the effects of speculation, reduce legal costs and permit a more rapid return on any investment. Localities which offer large blocks of land in one or a few titles will therefore be favoured over those where holdings are small and fragmented or where titles are shared by many individuals. Variations in land ownership and tenure may not only influence the location of tourist resorts but also their form and, in certain cases, the developer himself (Pearce, 1979b).

State land

New World mountain lands, in contrast to the long-settled alpine areas of Europe, are largely State controlled. Virtually all of the high country in New Zealand is Crown Land which is administered by different government departments. Although proceeding more cautiously at present, these departments have shown themselves to be reasonably receptive to ski-field development, with a variety of leases being given to both clubs and commercial developers (Pearce, 1978b), although in some cases concessions have not been granted. However, the conditions imposed by the lessors have influenced the form development has taken. Some park boards have resisted the opening of access roads. More importantly, no onfield commercial accommodation has been permitted, giving rise to a net separation between the ski-fields with uphill facilities and day shelters and nearby settlements which provide overnight accommodation. Coronet Peak and Queenstown are 19 km apart. A similar situation exists in Colorado (Thompson, 1971) where public land generally starts at the treeline and extends to the peaks. Uphill facilities have been permitted to be located there but the policies of the federal agencies have confined hotels, motels and cabins to the settlements in the valley bottoms and to other small enclaves of private land. Aspen and Vail, where this separation does not occur, are particularly successful resorts. However, as Simeral (1966) points out, leasing public land for the development of uphill facilities is generally less expensive than acquiring private land and may be particularly attractive where private tracts exist nearby on which to realize real estate operations.

Communal land

In the French Alps, the high mountain lands are traditionally communal pastures whereas the better land around the villages tends to consist of small, fragmented freehold properties. Administration of the communal pastures is usually vested in the local municipality and a promoter need deal only with a single body, often only the mayor himself, to obtain rights to these. Usually a contract is signed between the two, making available a small amount of land to be sold freehold for the construction of the resort itself, with a thirty-year concession of the ski-field (Perrin, 1971). This facility in obtaining rights to the communal pastures has been a significant factor contributing to the location of many of the new integrated resorts high above the level of traditional settlement (Reffay, 1974) and to their coherent, functional form.

Communalism, however, does not necessarily mean agreement within the unit as Nayacakalou (1972) points out in a different cultural context, that of Fiji. The different rights to the land are unevenly distributed amongst the owning groups, often giving rise to disputes over how a piece of land should be dealt with. Despite these complications, the Native Land Trust Board has developed a policy for the allocation of Fijian land for tourist development whereby the land owners are given the right to acquire a minimum of 10 per cent of the shares in the company which proposes to develop the site. Most hotels in Fiji to date, however, appear to have been built on alienated land belonging to expatriates.

Private land

Renard (1972) has demonstrated that in parts of France the system of tenure and the size of holdings effectively explain the distribution of second homes. Two basic tenurial systems exist along the Talmondais littoral (Vendee). Scattered amongst the large holdings of 30 to 60 hectares belonging mainly to absentee landlords and farmed by tenants, or 'metayers', are smaller owner-occupied holdings, often of less than 10 hectares and fragmented in many tiny plots clustered around the hamlets. It is these small plots which have been colonized by second home owners whereas almost without exception no tourist development has occurred on the large properties whose owners have preferred to retain their investment in the land. However, in north-western Sicily, where the Mafia are still active, Campagnoli-Ciaccio (1975) notes that absentee landlords have been quick to subdivide their large estates for second homes in order to reinvest their immediate gains in the city.

Although the decision to sell or retain one's property is generally a private matter, public intervention may force the decision in favour of tourist development. In France, if a promoter can show his project to be in the public interest, the authorities may expropriate private land on his behalf (Baretje and Defert, 1972). Such powers do not exist in Switzerland where private property remains sacred. As a result, individual chalets may be found on the ski slopes themselves, for example, at Verbier.

The price of land will of course be another major consideration. Where tourism is competing with other land uses, such as agriculture, industry or urbanization, prices will be much higher than where the land in question is not currently exploited, as may be the case with certain rural, upland or coastal areas. In urban areas in particular, different types of development will be able to support different land rents. More intensive forms such as high-rise hotels will be able to afford inner-city sites whereas camping grounds will be forced to locate on the outskirts.

Constraints and incentives

Tourist development may be limited by a variety of legal constraints in the form of building codes and zoning regulations. Some of these will be closely associated with the form of ownership; most national parks for example preclude private tourist dwellings and limit the amount of commercial accommodation. In many countries, the immediate foreshore is protected by measures such as the Crown chain, though much private ownership of the coastline is also evident. On a more local level, particularly in urban areas, zoning regulations may forbid the construction of particular forms of commercial accommodation in certain areas or influence the form it may take (e.g. height and size limitations).

Certain standards and regulations regarding the development of Crown land for cottaging, for example, are provided by the Ontario Ministry of Natural Resources (Priddle and Kreutzwiser, 1977, p. 171):

The policy specifies that a minimum of 25 per cent of the shoreline must be retained by the province for public access and use, and that where there is currently less than 25 per cent public ownership, no further cottage development on Crown land will take place. No cottage development will occur on islands of less than 3 acres (1.2 ha), on lakes of less than 100 acres (40 ha). . . . Design standards are also provided which require buildings to be set back 66 ft (20 m) from the high water line, a minimum lot width of 150 ft (46 m) and a minimum lot depth of 400 ft (122 m). Furthermore, all lots must have a view of the water.

On the other hand, to encourage regional development, governments may make available various development incentives (low interest loans, tax exemptions) in some regions and not others or selectively facilitate tourist development through provision of infrastructure or promotional assistance. Internationally, variations in public support for the tourist industry from one country to another may be a decisive locational influence (Mings, 1978b).

Other considerations

In addition to transport, plant and services, the presence or absence of other services and infrastructure in the form of health and security services, sewerage, power and water supply must also be taken into account. Spatial variations in the availability and cost of labour, the attitudes of residents to tourism and political stability will be other factors to bear in mind.

Carrying capacity

As Piperoglou (1967) has noted, before suitable regions or localities are developed they must be checked for their capacity to absorb tourists and new facilities and activities. Carrying capacity is the threshold of tourist activity beyond which facilities are saturated (physical capacity), the environment is degraded (environmental capacity) or visitor enjoyment is diminished (perceptual or psychological capacity). These concepts are now generally accepted but difficulties in measuring and quantifying the thresholds have restricted the use of carrying capacity as a planning tool (Barkham, 1973). Acceptable levels of crowding appear to differ from one society to another and physical and environmental carrying capacities can be affected by management techniques.

Some of these problems can be seen with regard to the carrying capacity of beaches. Firstly Table 3.2 shows a large range of recommended densities for determining their carrying capacity. Most of these refer to the perceptual capacity but clearly far higher densities are tolerated, perhaps even sought, by the gregarious tourists who flock to the beaches of the Riviera each summer.

One of the more useful methodological studies is that carried out at Brittas Bay in Ireland (An Foras Forbatha, 1973). Actual densities and distributions were obtained from aerial photographs taken on a Sunday in mid-summer. At the same time, the views of the beach users were sought in a questionnaire survey. Comparison of the two surveys suggested that many users would accept a density of 1,000 persons per hectare or 10 m² per person without considering a beach overcrowded.

Aerial photographs of developed beaches were also used in planning the scale of the new beach resorts in Languedoc-Roussillon. These suggested to the planners that about 600 holidaymakers per hectare of beach would be acceptable, that is, about 15 m² per person. Only the first 50 m from the water's edge were taken into account in calculating the area of beach. It was considered that not many people would go more than 50 m away in order to take advantage of the freshness of the sand and sea breezes and to supervise young children. Fortunately, the lack of tidal movement in the Mediterranean

Table 3.2 Recommended densities for determining the carrying capacity of beaches

Service d'etude d'aménagement touristique du littoral France.
  25 m² of beach per user for a 25 m wide zone, i.e. 1 user per linear metre of beach.
ACAU (1967)
  On average, 600 beach users per hectare, or more precisely:

No. of users	Width of beach		
Per linear metre of beach	20 m	33 m	50 m
average number			
– at one time	1.2	2.0	3.0
– the same day	2.5	4.0	6.0
maximum number			
– at one time	2.0	3.3	5.0
– the same day	4.0	6.5	10.0

Languedoc–Roussillon
  On average, 600 beach users per hectare, i.e. 15 m² per user.
Piperoglou (1966) – Greece
  Optimum use coefficient of beaches during peak periods.

Type of bay	Type of accommodation	m²/user
Small bay	High cost	20
Large bay	Medium cost	10
Long beach	Low cost	6.6

Park and Recreation Information System, California
  1,450 users per hectare, i.e. 7 m² per user.
Andric et al. (1962) – Yugoslavia
  5 m² per user.

does not complicate these calculations. Now these densities are only for a point in time but during the course of the day the beach population will change. Observation suggested that there were three waves of beach users during the day – in the morning, just after lunch and in the late afternoon. Also, some holidaymakers would not go to the beach at all on a given day. This figure was put arbitrarily at 25 per cent. Thus the daily capacity of the beach was estimated at:

  3 × 600 users/ha = 1,800/ha
  + 600 non-users = 2,400 resort residents per hectare of beach.

Therefore, for the 20 hectares of beach at La Grande Motte, it was decided to build not more than 48,000 beds.

   Many of the other carrying capacity studies are recorded in the bibliographies of Stankey and Lime (1973) and Baretje (1977).

SITE SELECTION AND REGIONAL RESOURCE EVALUATION TECHNIQUES

Two similar but distinct areas of planning and decision-making will involve a spatial differentiation of the factors discussed here. Firstly, it may be necessary to determine priorities for development amongst a given range of sites, that is, it is a question of site selection (Gearing and Var, 1977). Secondly, general evaluations for regional or national planning will require the identification and delimitation of those areas most suitable for one or more forms of tourist development (Piperoglou, 1967; Georgulas; 1970; Vedenin and Miroshnichenko, 1970; Lawson and Baud-Bovy, 1977; Var et al., 1977; Carvajal and Patri, 1979; Gunn, 1979).

Similar methodologies have been used in each case. These have usually involved the following basic steps:

(a) selection and possible weighting of criteria;
(b) evaluation of sites or areas in terms of these; and
(c) derivation of a relative measure of overall potential or attractiveness.

Few, if any, writers appear to have employed the full range of criteria discussed in the first section. Access and availability of land are the most frequently neglected. The land factor is of course very specific and may enter the decision-making process only after suitable broad areas have first been determined. Access, however, is far more critical. One of the few cases where access was emphasized was that of the Chilean Antarctic region (Carvajal and Patri, 1979). The criteria selected also depend on the specific objectives of the exercise. In their analysis of coastal locations in Turkey, Gearing and Var (1977) used six general factors – natural beauty, pollution level, historical value, distinctive local attractions, attitudes towards tourists, other recreative possibilities – and seven more specific ones affecting bathing – user density, water temperature, clarity and turbulence, wind factors, sand quality and beach descent. Different natural factors were used by Vedenin and Miroschnichenko (1970) in their recreational evaluation of Russia according to the season. For practical purposes, most of the writers have limited themselves to ten to twenty factors. However, it may be possible to incorporate a larger number of factors in a general evaluation by first reducing some to a single common index, as with climate or attractions. Care must be taken here for, as Gearing and Var stress, the factors should be independent and the attractivity indices of Piperoglou (1967) and Ferrario (1979) already include access and infrastructural components.

Having selected appropriate criteria these must then be weighted, for it is unlikely that each will be of equal value. Surveys of tourist preferences aid both in the selection of criteria and their weighting (Piperoglou, 1967; Ferrario, 1979). Such surveys are generally costly and may be inappropriate for assessing all factors; for example, access, infrastructure and land availability. Recourse to 'expert evaluation' is the most common solution (Gearing and Var, 1977; Var et al., 1977; Ritchie and Zins, 1978). Gunn (1979) simply assigns weights through arbitrary subjective selection. This is also probably the case for those others whose weighting procedures are not particularly clear. As well as this critical weighting of factors relative to each other, more attention could be given to a subsequent weighting based on the spatial coincidence of the various factors (Piperoglou, 1967; Ferrario, 1979).

A further question concerns the unit area of measurement for these criteria. Vedenin and Miroschnichenko (1970), for instance, employ the natural provinces of the USSR and Var et al. (1977) planning districts in British Columbia. The use of planning districts may be relevant where tourism is one of a number of development options but there is no inherent reason why tourist regions should correspond to any existing administrative units. The use of point data, where these are available and applicable, will therefore usually be the most appropriate, enabling tourist regions to be subsequently defined in terms of relevant parameters (Piperoglou, 1966; Ferrario, 1979).

Having determined the criteria which will discriminate between areas or sites with regard to their tourist potential, the regions or alternative sites in question must be evaluated in these terms. A basic approach is to rank them on some ordinal scale, not necessarily numerical; for instance, from most favourable to unfavourable (Vedenin and Miroschnichenko 1970; Gearing and Var, 1977). At this stage, certain regions or alternatives may be eliminated from further analysis through not attaining a designated threshold on key criteria; for example, climate or access. Gearing and Var also eliminate those sites which are 'dominated' by others, that is, those which consistently score lower on all criteria. To identify the most favourable regions, Vedenin and Miroschnichenko simply add the total number of points scored by each province on a five-point scale. Gearing and Var, however, employ a slightly more complicated 'quasi-lexicographic' procedure whereby alternatives scoring a maximum value on each criterion are given a score equal to that criterion's weight, the sum of these scores giving a composite score for each alternative. Other writers, however, score each alternative on every criterion used, not solely those attaining maximum values. Var *et al.* (1977) sought the co-operation of experts who were asked to evaluate districts with which they are familiar on a 0–100 scoring system. Average scores were multiplied by the criteria weights to give weighted total scores for each district. A similar approach is used by Carvajal and Patri (1979), in their study of the Chilean Antarctic region, only they appear to do their own evaluation using a much reduced scale (0–4), based mainly on the presence or absence of various conditions. As was noted earlier, Ferrario (1979) takes the number of mentions in guide books as a surrogate for expert evaluation of particular attractions.

Cartography is employed by other writers as an alternative to these essentially quantitative approaches (Lawson and Baud-Bovy, 1977; Gunn, 1979). This generally involves a thorough inventory of the region in question in terms of the criteria selected and the production of a corresponding series of maps. Synthesis may be achieved by the use of overlays to identify major tourist regions. Gunn, however, suggests the use of computer mapping incorporating the weighting of different factors and their aggregation into composite scores (Fig. 3.3). But as Piperoglou (1967) has shown, this may also be achieved through use of more conventional techniques.

A further approach is suggested by Georgulas (1970). He relies on the establishment of a classification system of different destination points. A number of functional elements are first identified. These are ranked according to a series of specific criteria (e.g. for first-class beaches, see above). A detailed notation system is then used to present information about each feature in tabulated form and cartographically. The clustering of features on the maps enables the identification of tourist regions.

Clearly the evaluation of the tourist potential of an area is a complex task and one where methodologies could be further developed and refined. A key problem is the comparison and weighting of a wide range of parameters, for as Nefedova *et al.* (1974, p. 507) point out: 'Any attempt to apply mathematical techniques to these multifactor evaluations without a sound basis for factor weighting is bound to fail in principle. But when factors can be logically weighted, quantitative techniques do assume significance.'

However, before techniques get too sophisticated or complicated it should be kept in mind that for the purposes of planning and most decision-making it is the relative importance of one location to another rather than absolute values which are initially important. At a subsequent stage, once initial choices have been made, the costing and economic analysis of particular sites, projects or regions will re-enter the process (Gearing and Var, 1977). Given that few private developers and most public authorities will not commit large sums for such exercises at the outset of the development process, techniques which offer a ready yet accurate assessment and which are not over-demanding in terms of data, time or money will prove the most practical.

Lack of finance or willingness to commit funds may be only one reason why full-scale evaluations are not carried out. Where the initiative is a local or even a regional one, the choice is likely to be restricted to nearby sites and attractions and any research will be to determine the feasibility of developing these. In such cases, the resultant pattern of development may be more a reflection of variations in enterprise than of the other factors outlined.

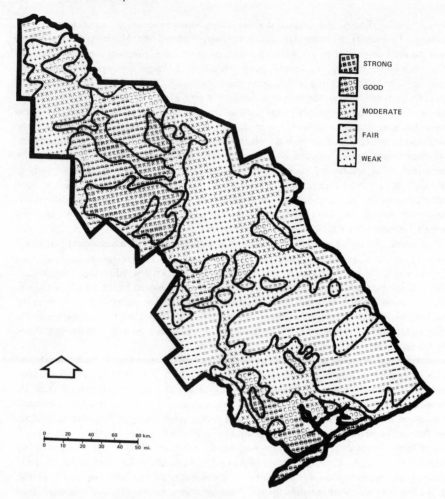

STRONG

GOOD

MODERATE

FAIR

WEAK

3.3   Sum of natural and cultural factors for touring potential
(20 counties in Texas).
(Gunn, 1979)

The basis of locational decision-making may also change through time. As Robertson
(1977, p. 122) points out in the case of second homes: 'The last buyers in a particular
second-home sub-division face a set of site characteristics that is quite different from
those faced by the first'. Similarly, someone wanting to open an aprés-ski facility will be
interested not so much in the physical characteristics of the ski-field but in the size and
nature of the market which the resort can provide.

Ski-field location

Ski-field location, perhaps more than any other type of tourism, is heavily dependent on
appropriate physical conditions, namely a good snow cover and suitable slopes.

Two main factors are important with regard to snow cover – the length of the season and the reliability of the snowfall. Longer seasons (of four to six months) and more reliable snowfalls will yield a more satisfactory and reliable return on investment in plant and infrastructure. Reliability will also build confidence amongst skiers. The duration of the snow cover is closely tied to altitude. At higher altitudes, say 2,000 m, the snowfall is generally not only greater, but the snow remains longer as temperatures are lower. Aspect and exposure to winds will also determine the amount of snow retention and the need for snow packing equipment. Duration of the snow cover is also a function of latitude; similar altitudes in the Pyrenees and the French Alps will experience different conditions. Martinelli (1976) stresses the importance of the early season snow cover as this is when demand is often the greatest and when the financial success or failure of many areas is decided. Other climatic parameters are also important. Wind conditions may not only influence retention of the snow but affect the functioning of lifts and the comfort of skiers. Likewise, temperature variations will affect the quality of the snow and the comfort of skiers as well as the design of buildings. Frequent fogs may lead to lengthy closures of the field. Sunshine is particularly important for the siting of resort accommodation but also a significant factor in skier enjoyment.

Resort ski-fields must offer a range of slopes to attract a variety of skiers. Rey (1968) suggests the following average slope angles are appropriate for the differing grades of skiers – beginners, less than 15°; intermediate, 15° – 25°; expert, more than 25°. The number of trails available and the total vertical drop are also important — experienced skiers will require a variety of slopes to ski during the day. Farwell (1970) proposes the total vertical drop be in the order of 1,500 vertical feet in the North-eastern United States and 3,000 to 4,000 vertical feet in the West. In France, the physical capacity of ski-fields is reckoned to be in the order of one skier per metre of vertical drop (Cumin, 1966). It is interesting to note that in her extensive study of three Aspen ski-fields, London (1979) found skiers' evaluations differed considerably from actual use statistics, suggesting marked differences between actual and perceived capacities. At the same time, a certain amount of flat stable land must be available close by to provide adequate building sites. Simeral (1966) suggests, as a general rule, 2 ha of base land for every 400 ha of hill operations, though this will depend on the form the resort takes (cf. La Plagne, Fig. 2.5).

France's Service d'Etude de l'Aménagement de la Montagne suggests an 'ideal' ski area would be a cirque, offering a variety of pistes, in terms of aspect and difficulty. These pistes would converge on a single reception area where the accommodation and other facilities would be built. Such a form gives skiers immediate access to all parts of the ski-field. These conditions are approached in several of the new resorts such as La Plagne, Pra Loup and Tignes. Ski-fields set in valleys are not generally accessible from a single centre, for example, Vars. On the other hand, access to them is generally easier than to the cirques which may require costly access roads.

The suitability of the physical conditions found above 2,000 m in the French Alps frequently coincides with the existence of communal pastures where rights to occupy the land can usually be obtained without too much difficulty. Elsewhere such sites may be on Crown or federal land where policies, while allowing development of lifts, may not permit the construction of accommodation and associated facilities.

The value of any one site will increase where the possibility of linkages with other ski-fields exist, for skiers, more than their coastal counterparts, seek variety on their holidays. A location within or near to an already well established and known ski area will be favoured over a more isolated one. Thus, Aime 2,000 forms part of the La Grande Plagne complex which in turn is favourably situated in the Tarentaise. Proximity to summer attractions or resorts is another advantage. Real estate sales may benefit from this double season or the ski-field may profit from existing infrastructure and accommodation. Chamonix, for example, developed first as a summer resort and the summer traffic still exceeds that of the winter (Veyret-Verner, 1972).

Proximity to the market is another key factor. As Stansfield (1973, p. 6) points out in the case of New Jersey's ski industry; 'It is apparent that otherwise mediocre slopes in combination with hazardously unpredictable local climate conditions can, if accessible to population centres, easily be transformed into a successful ski recreation area.' Access and proximity to urban areas is especially important for those centres catering for day visitors and week-end skiers, as is the case with most Canterbury (New Zealand) ski-fields (Pearce, 1978b). Vacation resorts, on the other hand, may be more distant but will need to offer a wider range of facilities and generally better skiing conditions. In a detailed study of Grenoble skiers, Keogh (1980) shows the 'sporting' skier gives more weight to the length of ski runs in selecting his ski-field whereas the 'social' skier is more concerned by the cost of lift tickets. Parnell (1974), in his planning report on the prospect of winter sports development at Fort William, provides a good example in a British context of how these various factors are evaluated.

Conclusions

A wide variety of factors must be taken into account when evaluating tourist resources. The importance of each of these will vary from situation to situation depending on the type of tourism being developed and the context and stage of development. Even in the more specific case of ski-fields, different factors assume different emphasis according to location and the type of skier being catered for. However, the range of evaluation and selection techniques reviewed do provide a good basis for assessing and ordering these factors although there is still scope for refining these techniques further.

CHAPTER 4
ANALYSING THE IMPACT OF TOURIST DEVELOPMENT

Considerable debate exists today over the nature and extent of the impact which tourist development may have on host societies and localities (UNESCO, 1976). Tourism is no longer seen as being unreservedly beneficial and costs as well as benefits are now attributed to its development (Young, 1973; Bryden, 1973). Initially seen mainly in economic terms, assessment of the impact of tourism has been broadened to include environmental (Cohen, 1978) and social-cultural considerations (Smith, 1977b; de Kadt, 1979).

Much of the conflict in the literature arises from the fact that different writers have argued their case from their own particular standpoint. Economists, at least in the 1960s, tended to emphasize economic gains to the exclusion of all else. Anthropologists and sociologists, on the other hand, have generally been more pessimistic, stressing the socially disruptive nature of tourism. These disciplinary differences have often been compounded by weak methodologies and a certain degree of emotionalism (Turner and Ash, 1975). There has been a general failure to recognize that tourism may develop in different ways (Ch. 2) and that even similar processes may give rise to widely different impacts when the context differs. Mings (1978c, p. 30) goes so far as to state that: 'our inadequate understanding of the varied impacts of tourism development has contributed to both unwarranted optimism and excessive negativism among public officials'. This chapter attempts to provide a general framework for assessing the impact of tourism before examining in more detail the environmental, social/cultural and economic issues involved and the more specific techniques for analysing these.

A GENERAL FRAMEWORK FOR IMPACT ASSESSMENT

To date, most studies on the impact of tourism have been concerned with development which has already occurred. However, with the emergence during the 1970s of environmental impact auditing procedures in the United States, New Zealand and elsewhere, a new kind of impact assessment has emerged, that of appraising the likely effects of development before a project goes ahead. As Phillips (1974, p. 63) notes: 'in theory at least, the burden of proof now falls on the person or group wishing to disturb the environment. It is necessary for them to show that the proposed action will not impair environmental quality or that the social benefits of the action will outweigh the social costs'.

Potter (1978) presents a very useful methodology for impact assessment, based partly on the experience of analysing the impact of oil drilling platform construction in Scotland. Potter's methodology, when broadened and modified to consider not only environmental but also social and economic impacts, provides an extremely good framework for investigating the impact of tourist development. Moreover, it can be usefully applied to both future projects and those which have already taken place (Table 4.1). The basic steps (1–9) described below are involved.

Table 4.1   A general framework for assessing the impact of tourism (After Potter, 1978).

1 Examine context – environment, society, economy.
2 Forecast future if tourist development does not proceed/had not proceeded.
3 Examine tourist development.
4 Forecast future if development proceeds/examine what happened when development occurred.
5 Identify in quantitative and qualitative terms differences between 2 and 4.
6 Suggest amelioration measures to reduce adverse impacts.
7 Analyse the impacts and compare alternatives.
8 Present the results.
9 Make a decision.

1. Examine context – environment, society, economy

The first step is to examine the context of development, either that which existed prior to the advent of tourism or the contemporary situation where the concern is with the study of potential impact.

Physical environment   In order to gauge its resiliency and suitability for development, the environment must be examined in terms of its physical characteristics – soil, vegetation, relief, aspect, fauna, climate – and the dynamics of the relationships between these. Attention, for example, must be paid to slope or dune stability, run-off characteristics and the resiliency of biotic communities. As well as a general environmental assessment, micro-level studies must also be undertaken, for example, determining the precise location of avalanche corridors. In the case of a built environment, attention must be directed at the nature, scale, form and location of existing buildings and street patterns as well as existing land uses.

Society   Characteristics of the host society to be taken into account include population size; demographic composition and vitality; ethnic, social or religious structure. For example, is the population increasing or decreasing, is it composed of more than one ethnic group, what social customs are evident? As White (1974, pp. 35–6) notes, such social/demographic characteristics can have a significant influence on the degree of development and change: 'a strong area can sustain the capitalisation and provision of labour from within itself, while a weak area is immediately more susceptible to outside economic influences in the form of external investment and immigration, so that the local socio-cultural structure is quickly changed'.

Economy   The size, diversity and vitality of the economy at various scales – national, regional or local – are further factors which need to be considered. The economy in question may be well developed, developing, depressed or in decline. It may be broadly based or heavily reliant on a single sector, a strong economy or a dependent one. Tourism may already be a significant sector or totally unimportant. These factors will influence the extent of local participation and degree of external involvement as well as determine the costs and benefits to different sectors of society and the ultimate impact of tourism.

2. Forecast future if tourist development does not proceed/had not proceeded

Having examined the existing situation and having established contemporary trends, the next step is to predict what would happen/would have happened if tourism does not develop/had not developed. This may involve a projection of demographic and economic trends. What would have happened, for example, to the alpine communities discussed in Chapter 2 had tourism not been developed?

3. Examine project

As has been stressed earlier, it is essential not to think of tourist development as merely the growth of some monolithic phenomenon known simply as tourism. Each particular project or development must be examined in terms of the range of specific elements and the process characteristics outlined in Chapter 2. What precisely is being developed, by whom, for whom, how, when, where and why are the fundamental questions which must be asked here. The question of timing, for example, is critical. Where tourism develops gradually over a number of years there will be a longer period for social and environmental adjustment and local participation may be increased as needs in terms of labour, supplies and capital will be met more readily by local resources. Where rapid development occurs, there may be apparently greater immediate returns but it will be unlikely that the host community can respond to such demands and provide all that is needed so that, in the medium and long term, 'leakages' from the area may be large, effectively reducing benefits to the community.

4. Forecast future if development proceeds/examine what resulted when development occurred

What parts of the environment, segments of society and sectors of the economy will be affected/have been affected, by what (specifically), in what ways and to what extent are the principal questions to be asked next. The impacts of past developments will usually be assessed more readily than future impacts can be predicted, particularly if the conditions existing before the advent of tourism have been satisfactorily established. Comparison with past developments will also be useful in assessing future impacts, keeping in mind, of course, the effect of differing contexts and types of development.

5. Identify in quantitative and qualitative terms differences between steps 2 and 4.

To be able to fully evaluate the impact of tourist development the difference between tourism developing and it not developing must be assessed, that is, the difference between the results of steps 2 and 4. This involves measurement of a wide range of parameters in quantitative terms and a more general qualitative assessment of others. What should be examined and how are questions which have been subject to a certain amount of debate and answered with varying degrees of success. Two associated problems arise – the techniques to be used and the availability of appropriate data and information. Data deficiencies are very common, particularly in studies of past developments, for as Figuerola (1976) points out, there is often a shortage of even the most basic statistics. In general there are few earlier reports to draw upon or with which to compare the present. A further difficulty arises here in comparing the different types of impact. Whereas economic costs and benefits may be presented in purely dollar terms, social and environmental issues cannot usually be expressed so conveniently. Problems may also arise in establishing the causal links between different facets of development and changes in the host society or environment. It might be shown rather readily that new employment opportunities have arisen out of the development of tourist facilities but accompanying changes in the economic aspirations and behaviour of these workers may be due as much to external influences (such as the mass media) as to direct experience of the tourist industry. Various techniques used for examining the different impacts of tourism are described more fully below.

6. Suggest amelioration measures to reduce adverse impacts

Having identified sources of adverse impact, various measures might be suggested to reduce these. Spatially, for example, two broad strategies might be adopted – concentration or dispersal of tourist activity (see Ch. 5). The seasonal concentration of tourism is a further problem and a staggering of holidays may alleviate social and environmental pressures and lead to a more balanced economy. More specific suggestions might be to relocate facilities, increase the capacity of sewage treatment plants or to limit the activities of visitors through zoning.

7. Analyse the impacts and compare alternatives (where available).

Where alternatives exist, the merits of each case should be assessed and their impacts compared. Basically, two sets of alternatives may be identified. Firstly, there may be alternative sites available for a specific project, for example, the development of a new ski-field. Is site A more environmentally stable than site B? Secondly, in a particular context, a range of development possibilities may exist. Overall, is project X more desirable than project Y? In addition, it may also be necessary to compare the impact of tourism with other development strategies if a range of choices exists. What will be/would have been the impact of developing forestry or expanding agriculture instead of tourism?

8. Present the results

The results of the various studies should then be presented as clearly, concisely and objectively as possible. In the interests of a broad audience and a more ready comprehension of the results, technical jargon, complex formulae and the like should be reduced to a minimum or confined to appendices.

9. Make a decision

ASSESSING THE ENVIRONMENTAL IMPACT OF TOURISM

Assessment of the environmental impact of tourism is particularly important, for the various facets of the environment constitute the basis of much tourist development (see Ch. 3). Moreover, tourism tends to be attracted to some of the more fragile environments; for example, small islands, coastal zones, alpine areas and centres of historical or cultural interest.

Recognizing both the need to maintain a sound environment and the mounting pressures from the expansion of tourism, the Organization for Economic Co-operation and Development (OECD) established a research programme in 1977 and 1978 to investigate these issues. To ensure comparability for case studies to be prepared by member countries, a series of guidelines was prepared and a general research framework was presented (Table 4.2). Table 4.2 identifies a number of tourist-generated stressor activities, the associated stresses, subsequent environmental responses and man's reactions to these, both individually and collectively. Stress has been defined as: 'the strain imposed on peo-

Table 4.2 A framework for the study of tourism and environmental stress (After OECD).

STRESSOR ACTIVITIES	STRESS	PRIMARY RESPONSE ENVIRONMENTAL	SECONDARY RESPONSE (REACTION) HUMAN
1. *Permanent environmental restructuring* (a) Major construction activity urban expansion transport network tourist facilities marinas, ski-lifts, sea walls (b) Change in land use expansion of recreational lands	Restructuring of local environments expansion of built environments land taken out of primary production	Change in habitat Change in population of biological species Change in health and welfare of man Change in visual quality	*Individual* – impact on aesthetic values *Collective measures* expenditure on environmental improvements expenditure on management of conservation designation of wild life conservation and national parks controls on access to recreational lands
2. *Generation of waste residuals* urbanization transportation	Pollution loadings emissions effluent discharges solid waste disposal noise (traffic, aircraft)	Change in quality of environmental media air water soil Health of biological organisms Health of humans	*Individual defensive measures* Locals air conditioning recycling of waste materials protests and attitude change Tourists change of attitude towards the environment decline in tourist revenues *Collective defensive measures* expenditure of pollution abatement by tourist related industries clean-up of rivers, beaches
3. *Tourist activities* skiing walking hunting trail bike riding collecting	Trampling of vegetation and soils Destruction of species	Change in habitat Change in population of biological species	*Collective defensive measures* expenditure on management of conservation designation of wildlife conservation and national parks controls on access to recreational lands
4. *Effect on population dynamics* Population growth	Population density (seasonal)	Congestion Demand for natural resources land and water energy	*Individual* – Attitudes to overcrowding and the environment *Collective* Growth in support services, e.g. water supply, electricity

ple and their enjoyment of amenities or on resources, the impact of which can be objectively measured or may be subjectively experienced in the light of defined values'. The emphasis here is on measurable stress and on linking specific stresses and responses to particular activities.

The first major source of environmental stress is permanent restructuring of the environment brought about by a variety of major construction activities, such as new urban developments, construction of highways and the building of marinas or ski-lifts. Clearly, the replacement of a natural environment such as a stretch of coast or a valley bottom by a new built environment will have a variety of far-reaching and long-lasting results in terms of the existing biological species and physical conditions in the area. In some cases, man's response to the stress created may subsequently alleviate some of the problems. Bayfield (1974), for example, notes the decline in accelerated erosion resulting from the construction of new chair-lifts on Cairngorm after the damaged ground was reseeded and drains were provided. In addition to these physical changes, there may be significant changes in visual amenity. Several writers (Eckbo, 1969; Relph, 1976) have commented on the 'homogenizing' influence of tourism: 'modern mobility tends to cancel out one reason for its existence by making alike all those places that once attracted by their differences' (Eckbo, 1969, p. 29).

A second major area of stress is that resulting from the generation of new or increased waste residuals. One of the most interesting studies on air pollution in resort communities is that by Kirkpatrick and Reeser (1976) on Aspen and Vail (Colorado). Their study emphasizes the importance of context in impact studies. It was demonstrated that mountain altitude and terrain features in Vail and Aspen seriously inhibited air pollution dispersion as compared to Denver and the Colorado Plains. Moreover, automobile emissions were found to be higher in mountain communities (as a result of the effects of altitude and slower travelling speeds), as were particulate emissions due to the large scale use of open fireplaces for heating and social effect. As a result of these factors it was shown that for similar populations, in terms of carbon monoxide, the air quality at Vail is about ten times as fragile as that in Denver.

However, in terms of waste residuals, the most widespread problem in resort communities is water pollution through the discharge of inadequately treated effluent. Seas, lakes, rivers and other water bodies which are among the most attractive resources for tourist development are also frequently used for the cheap and convenient disposal of sewage. This practice may in time give rise to the eutrophication of these water bodies through an increase in discharged phosphates or contamination such that human health may be seriously impaired and/or natural flora and fauna destroyed. The 'collapse' of the Millstatter Lake in Austria during the early 1970s following a tenfold increase in the tourist traffic in the preceding two decades and restrictions on bathing in certain Mediterranean beaches, are cases in point. These examples also emphasize the tourism/environment relationship. Whereas industrial discharges, for example from chemical ·plants, would have little effect on that industry, closure of beaches or serious changes in the aesthetic qualities of lakes may result in a significant downturn in the tourist traffic. Although the fragility of these environments is important, the problem here is basically one of management and stems essentially from an inadequate infrastructure. This may result from the rapid expansion of tourism wherein construction of accommodation outstrips the provision of treatment facilities. More commonly it arises simply from a basic inability or unwillingness of local authorities to finance the necessary sewerage plant. Once this financial handicap is overcome the situation can usually be reversed and this source of stress considerably reduced. Economically, as well as environmentally, provision of adequate infrastructure from the outset will in the long run prove less expensive than the correction of environmental damage plus the eventual construction of the necessary plant.

The best documented aspect of environmental impact is that concerning recreational activities, although most of these studies refer more to picnic grounds, national parks and wilderness areas rather than to resorts as such (Wall and Wright, 1977). Many of these have been concerned with the trampling effects on soils and vegetation by various activities such as skiing (Baiderin, 1978), trail-bike riding (Crozier *et al.*, 1978) and walking (Liddle, 1975) in a range of environments including dunes (Usher *et al.* 1974) coral reefs (Woodland and Hooper, 1977) and forests and meadows (Dale and Weaver, 1974, 1978). The effects of these activities include an increase in soil compaction and erosion, changes in plant cover and species diversity. Again, attention to spatial variation at the local scale is important. Usher *et al.* (1974), for example, note in their study of a Yorkshire coastal reserve that although the main attraction, the beaches, were themselves resistant to pressure, this was not the case with the dunes which first had to be crossed. Habitat changes can subsequently affect wildlife, and together with other recreational effects such as disturbance and destruction may set in train a further series of impacts (Fig. 4.1).

A fourth associated area of impact is the effect of tourist development on population dynamics, especially seasonal increases in population and population densities. One of the more obvious effects of such seasonal increases is the resultant physical congestion experienced in many areas, be they beaches, ski slopes or historic centres. Overseas tourist arrivals in New Zealand, for example, are highest from October to March, which coincides with New Zealand's peak domestic holiday season. However, in some urban areas the effect of the influx of tourists may be lessened by the outflow of local holidaymakers, for example as several million Parisians head for the coast or countryside in July and August. Seasonal influxes will also increase the demand for natural resources such as water and energy and contribute to some of the effects already noted; for example, the generation of waste residuals.

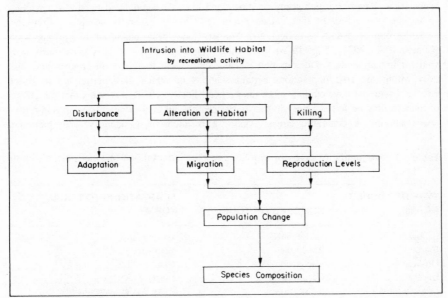

4.1 The impacts of recreation on wildlife.
(Wall and Wright, 1977)

Three major sets of techniques for analysing these various impacts in detail may be identified: after-the-fact analyses, the monitoring of change through time and simulation methods (Wall and Wright, 1977). Each has associated problems and advantages and may be more appropriate for some types of studies than others. After-the-fact studies, for example, require a sound knowledge of conditions prior to development. Wall and Wright suggest that such an approach is more suitable for soil and vegetation studies than for those of water quality and wildlife where it may be more difficult to establish controls. Monitoring can be very useful, particularly in allowing the simultaneous study of both cause (tourist development) and effect. Simulation studies, for example of trampling, can be especially helpful in predicting future impacts. Certain types of impact are more readily measured than others. Coliform counts or atmospheric particulate levels can be established rather more easily than levels of visual pollution.

Tourist development, of course, does not give rise solely to negative impact (Cohen, 1978). Much development, for the tourist at least, may enhance his appreciation of the environment. The construction of roads or cableways will give him greater access to viewpoints or open up new ski-fields; the provision of accommodation facilities will enable him to stay in the area. More generally, tourism may be the means of preserving areas of scenic beauty or centres of historical interest by providing an economic or social rationale to reinforce purely environmental or historical considerations. Such considerations in the past have often proved insufficient by themselves.

THE SOCIAL AND CULTURAL IMPACT OF TOURIST DEVELOPMENT

A prime consideration in examining the social and cultural impact of tourist development is the nature and composition of the various groups involved and the relationships between these. The basic dichotomy of 'hosts and guests', popularized by the recent comprehensive publication of that name (Smith, 1977b), is generally accepted. However, neither group is usually homogenous. Tourists have been classified in various ways (Cohen, 1972, 1974; Plog, 1973), but Smith's typology (Table 4.3) is particularly relevant for impact studies. Demographic, social, ethnic and linguistic differences may also exist within the host population, certain sections of which may participate in or be affected by tourist development more than others. Fuster (1974) also notes that the effects of tourism may be felt not only in the tourist centres but also in neighbouring non-tourist towns and in the generating areas. Again, it is important to identify what particular

Table 4.3 Frequency of types of tourists and their adaptations to local norms (Smith, 1977b)

TYPE OF TOURIST NORMS	NUMBERS OF TOURISTS	ADAPTATIONS TO LOCAL NORMS
Explorer	Very limited	Accepts fully
Elite	Rarely seen	Adapts fully
Off-beat	Uncommon but seen	Adapts well
Unusual	Occasional	Adapts somewhat
Incipient mass	Steady flow	Seeks Western amenities
Mass	Continuous influx	Expects Western amenities
Charter	Massive arrivals	Demands Western amenities

groups or segments of society are experiencing what specific effects of tourist development. The social impact of tourism will vary according to the differences between the
visitors and the visited, whether in terms of numbers, race, culture or social outlook.
Lundgren (1972, p. 94), observes that in general: 'the force of tourist-generated local
impact seems to increase with distance from the generating country'.

Several specific characteristics of tourism must also be kept in mind. Firstly, the
transitory nature of the relationships between hosts and guests, often coupled with language barriers, allows little opportunity for understanding to develop between the two
groups. Secondly, the fact that the tourist is on holiday while the host is at work may
heighten differences between the two, especially as holiday behaviour is generally much
less restrained than usual. Thirdly, the seasonal nature of much tourism tends to be more
disruptive than year-round activities, often creating the need for seasonal workers and
exacerbating any tensions which might exist between the different groups. Finally, the
outward signs of tourism may be more manifest than other types of development; for
example, agricultural reform or the introduction of television. As a result, effects which
have their origins elsewhere may be attributed to tourism. At worst, the industry may
become the general scapegoat for any and every social malaise.

Table 4.4 summarizes many of the social and cultural impacts which tourist
development may have on host societies. Firstly, tourism may affect the demographic
structure of those populations. Development of the industry will usually affect the size of
the resident population, as the creation of new jobs slows out-migration or attracts new
workers to the area (Dumas, 1975). Ultimately there may even be a significant change in

Table 4.4 The social and cultural impacts of tourism (After Figuerola, 1976).

(a) Impact on population structure:
  size of population;
  age/sex composition;
  modification of family size;
  rural → urban transformation of population.
(b) Transformation of forms and types of occupation:
  impact on/of language and qualification levels;
  impact on occupational distribution by sector;
  demand for female labour;
  increase in seasonality of employment.
(c) Transformation of values:
  political;
  social;
  religious;
  moral.
(d) Influence on traditional way of life:
  on art, music and folklore;
  on habits and customs;
  on daily living.
(e) Modification of consumption patterns:
  qualitative alterations;
  quantitative alterations.
(f) Benefits to the tourist:
  relaxation, recuperation, recreation;
  change of environment;
  widening of horizons;
  social contact

the degree of regional urbanization. This process tends to be age and sex selective, thereby altering the composition of the population as well as its size. Greater occupational mobility may also reduce family ties leading to the break-down of the extended family (Greenwood, 1972).

Other occupational changes may stem from tourist development. Language can be a critical factor in determining which sectors of the population will profit from tourism. Many native spectacles, for example, are presented by expatriate entrepreneurs or organized by the better-educated indigenes, the so-called 'culture brokers'. White (1974) has shown a more general decline in Romansch speaking in a multi-lingual area of Switzerland as tourism has developed there. The prospect of good jobs in the tourist industry may increase the desire for educational attainment. However, if initially the demand for qualified staff exceeds local capabilities or if control is in the hands of external promoters, then the better positions will be filled from outside, leaving the local residents the more menial tasks. Continuation of this policy will lead to frustration and perhaps hostility towards tourism. Employment opportunities in tourism may draw workers from other sectors of the economy – for example, agriculture – with consequent effects on class or social structure. Elsewhere, jobs which previously had no cash return in many societies, such as cooking and cleaning, may now become income earning if performed in hotels, thus altering the status of these workers, particularly of women. Resorts dependent on significant influxes of seasonal workers may suffer from a lack of social stability, the constant turnover in the population allowing little time for lasting relationships or community spirit to develop. Added to this are the work patterns of the tourist industry, often characterized by long hours and split shifts. On the other hand, some, particularly the younger seasonal workers, may be attracted by the excitement and interest of continually meeting new people.

Values may be transformed through the bringing together of different groups of people, even if at times only very briefly. This is commonly known as the 'demonstration effect'. On the Greek island of Myconos, for example, the sociologist Lambiri-Dimaki (1976) notes the: 'democratization and modernization of attitudes' among the young, arising out of contact with youthful Western tourists. In this case it was the observed behaviour of the visitors, especially the equality of the females, which was as important as direct contact between the local residents and the tourists. Elsewhere, tourist behaviour may be offensive to local norms as with the arrival of hordes of scantily-clad foreigners on the beaches of conservative and Catholic Spain. Increased prostitution is commonly associated with an expansion of tourism but little research has been carried out in this area. Jones (1978), in his brief study of prostitution in Bali, concludes that prostitution is usually changed, not caused, by tourist demand. The 'beach boy – Canadian secretary syndrome' suggests sex roles are reversed in the Caribbean. In some cases, it is the tourist who is influenced the most. This is especially the case with those seeking to reinforce or expand their political, ideological or religious beliefs by visits to such places as Israel, India, Cuba, Mecca and Lourdes. The oft-cited increase in world-wide understanding resulting from international tourism is perhaps exaggerated, given the nature and duration of tourist – host contact. On the other hand, there is little evidence to suggest any damage to international relations and any benefits, however small, must surely be welcome in this domain.

The impact of tourism on traditional life styles is especially important where those traditions form the basis for the development of tourism. Ethnic tourism is particularly a feature of the Third World but the arts in general have been, and still are, a very significant part of Europe's appeal to the traveller. Basically two differing schools of thought and bodies of evidence exist (Smith, 1977b). Tourism is held by some observers to have a corrupting influence, brought about by the cheapening of artistic values or the commercialization of local traditions and customs; for example, the performance of religious or historical ceremonies on demand, out of context and for monetary reward. Other writers suggest tourists can have a strengthening and stimulating effect, either by reawakening interest in a society's own culture or simply by supporting the ballet, theatre or museums by their presence and entrance fees. Tourism may also impose other more banal but no less significant pressures on host populations, as when visitors are served ahead of local residents in shops and the latter are jostled in the streets during the height of the season, or restricted from the use of certain beaches.

The demonstration effect noted earlier also encompasses daily patterns of consumption. Emulating the visitors, the residents may adopt new clothing styles, begin eating and drinking the imported food and beverages favoured by the tourist or aspire to obtain the transistor radios, cameras and other material goods so casually displayed by him. Inability by the local to emulate the visitor, if so desired, may lead to a greater awareness of poverty, envy, frustration and consequent ill-will towards the visitor or to his compatriots who have been more successful. At the same time, fulfilment of the desire for more imported goods may have significant adverse economic effects.

Finally, there are the benefits of the holiday to the tourist himself. Although experienced at the destinations, the benefits may be most felt at home, where a phase of eager anticipation precedes and a period of fond recollection follows the holiday itself. The social 'need' for holidays is now being increasingly experienced (Social Tourism Study Group, 1976) and forms the rationale for the policies of social tourism being adopted by a growing number of countries (Lanquar and Raynouard, 1978).

The objective assessment of these varied impacts is clearly no easy task. Certain impacts lend themselves more readily to measurement than others. Providing the data are available, and many censuses do provide the basic information, the demographic and, to a lesser extent, the occupational changes can be measured without too much difficulty. This is also so with certain changes in consumption patterns, as measured by import statistics or food intake levels, or other indicators such as language (White, 1974) and art (Graburn, 1976). Less readily assessed are value changes and social modifications. Attitude surveys have yielded useful information on types of impact (Cant, 1978; Pizam, 1978; Rothman, 1978) although there are often problems in separating actual changes from perceived ones. Measurement over time is also difficult unless surveys are carried out at regular intervals. With this research there is also an ever present danger of the researcher's own biases intruding. Whether the liberalization of certain attitudes is good or bad depends to a large extent on the researcher's own point of view. Then too there is the difficulty of filtering out the impact of other external factors, for example, the demonstration effect of films, the press or returned migrant workers.

ESTIMATING THE ECONOMIC IMPACT OF TOURIST DEVELOPMENT

The objective and detailed evaluation of the economic impact of tourism can be a long and complicated task. Much of the complexity arises out of the disparate nature of the industry and the range of benefits and costs which can accrue to or are borne by various groups or individuals. Figure 4.2 attempts to provide a general framework by which to approach this problem by identifying systematically the different issues and relationships involved. For either the development or operational phase, the emphasis is on relating particular costs and benefits to specific aspects of development and to particular groups of people.

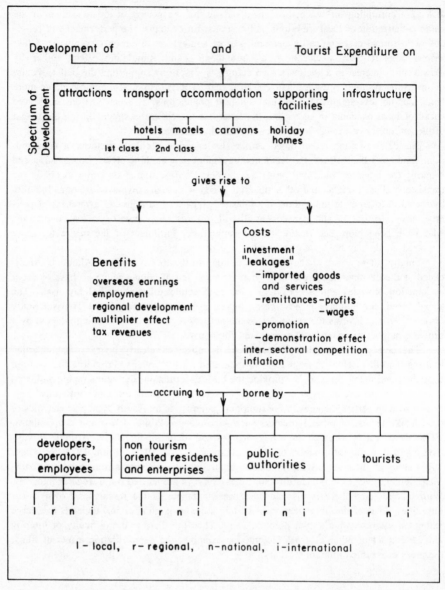

4.2 A framework for assessing the economic impact of tourist development.

Development vs operation

It is first of all useful to distinguish between the developmental stage, that is when plant and facilities are being constructed, and the operational stage, when they are being used by the visitor. In the first phase, most of the capital will be that of the developers (or their financiers). In the second, it will largely be tourist expenditure which is circulating in the economy. The transition from one stage to the next may be accompanied by differing costs and benefits. Much of the local impact from second homes comes from the initial sale of land with little subsequent job creation or spending in the area by the second home owners (Barbier, 1977). State expenditure on infrastructure may initially be very heavy but some expenses will be recuperated in the long term, for example, through increased tax revenues (Fuster, 1974). Thus the stage at or time period during which a project is examined may influence significantly its economic evaluation.

The spectrum of development

Secondly, it is important to consider the whole spectrum of the tourist project or industry (see Ch. 2). There has been a tendency for impact studies to focus on the accommodation sector, perhaps because it is the most evident. Table 4.5 shows that accommodation is indeed the single largest item of tourist expenditure in many countries. Elsewhere, for example in Hong Kong and Panama, shopping is the major item of expenditure. To concentrate on accommodation along here would be clearly to under-estimate tourism's contribution to the economy. Moreover, accommodation tends to be more capital intensive than other sectors of the industry, giving rise to differing costs and benefits.

Within each sector it is also necessary to detail the particular type of development, for instance, to distinguish between the different accommodation possibilities. A comprehensive economic survey of the Greater Tayside region of Scotland (Henderson, 1975) showed that for every 10,000 tourist days spent in the region, thirteen job opportunities were created there. However, hotel users were found to be responsible for more than twice this average amount (twenty-eight regional jobs per 10,000 hotel user days) while those using self-catering accommodation generated an average of approximately nine jobs. Moreover, distinction between types of hotels may also be critical. Large luxury hotels will require heavier capital investments and may generate more jobs per room, but their investment/job ratio may well be less than that of smaller, more modest hotels (Elkan, 1975). Likewise, the pattern of costs and benefits for uphill facilities in a ski resort, for instance, will differ from that of the provision of 'après-ski' entertainment.

Costs and benefits

The main economic benefits which tourist development may bring were outlined in Chapter 2 in terms of the motives for developing tourism. These benefits are accompanied by a series of costs, often in the form of 'leakages' from the area in question. The economic impact of tourism is thus the balance between these benefits and the associated costs.

Balance of payments

At a national level, the major aim of both developed and developing countries in promoting international tourism is commonly to increase overseas earnings, to improve or redress the balance of payments situation. France's Fifth Five Year Plan (1966–70) is a good example: 'the tourism policy will have as its fundamental objective during the course of the 5th Plan to reverse this trend (towards a deficit) by giving priority to the most profitable investment in terms of overseas earnings, whether this be in the short or long term'.

Development of international tourism offers three main advantages for increasing overseas earnings:

1. It has been, and still is, a growth industry.
2. The tourism market, unlike that for many manufactured or primary goods, is relatively little protected. Moreover it is a market which comes to the producer.
3. For many countries, tourism may represent a diversification of the economy.

Table 4.5 Tourist expenditure patterns in selected countries, 1974 *Economic Review of World Tourism*, WTO, Table 43, p. 64, 1976)

COUNTRY	TOTAL EXPENDITURE (millions of $US)	ACCOMMODATION (%)	MEALS (%)
Bahamas	327.9	43.4	14.7
Brazil	66.7	30	28
Dahomey	1.6	48	27
Ecuador	22.64	34.8	17.4
Hong Kong	476.0	15.3	9.3
Israel	130.6	44	18
Panama	94.4	22.8	7

Globally, international tourism accounts for about 4 per cent of total world trade, according to (WTO) estimates, but its contribution to the export earning of many individual countries, both developed and developing, is much higher (see Table 4.6). These figures,

Table 4.6 International tourist receipts for selected countries, 1975 (WTO, *Tourist Compendium*, 1977, Table 5.6, pp. 128–9)

COUNTRY	RECEIPTS (MILLIONS OF $US)	TOURISM RECEIPTS (AS % OF EXPORTS)
Jordan	114.3	74.7
Malta	75.7	45.3
Spain	3,404.2	44.3
Panama	103.5	38.0
Tunisia	280.4	32.7
Morocco	434	28.1
Greece	621.5	27.2
Austria	2,781.3	24.0
Kenya	93.5	19.6
Yugoslavia	768.4	18.9
Jamaica	128.7	17.6
Israel	233.3	12.7
Switzerland	1,606	12.4
Italy*	2,372.9	10.7
New Zealand	160.7	7.5
Great Britain	2,442	5.6
France*	1,923.3	5.4
United States of America	4,876	4.6
West Germany	2,900.4	3.2
Netherlands	1,108	3.2
Australia	300	2.6
Sweden	342	2.0
Poland	163.3	1.6
Zambia	12.8	1.6
Brazil	71.2	0.8
Ghana	1.2	0.2

* 1973

LOCAL TRANSPORT (%)	RECREATION (%)	SHOPPING (%)	OTHER (%)
7.8	14.1	13.4	6.7
11	14	9	8
12	3	9	1
8.7	17.4	17.4	4.3
2.1	5.9	59.4	8.0
16	2	18	2
4.8	72	43.5	14.7

however, say little about the net contribution of tourism to the balance of payments position of any particular country. A common though somewhat misleading attempt to rectify this is to subtract expenditure by outgoing nationals from the sums brought into the country by foreign visitors. This is largely spurious reasoning in that the two sums are fairly independent of each other (Gray, 1970). The net balance of payments contribution from international tourism can be calculated more accurately by relating expenditure by foreign tourists to associated costs. These costs and leakages may take several forms (IUOTO, 1975):

1. The costs of imported goods and services used by tourists; for example, imported fruit or whiskey.
2. The foreign exchange costs of capital investment in tourist facilities.
3. Payments abroad in the form of:
   (a) profits and capital remittances by foreign tourist companies;
   (b) wage remittances by expatriate workers;
   (c) interest payments on foreign loans;
   (d) management, royalties and other fees, e.g. for franchised hotels;
   (e) payments due to foreign travel agents and tour operators.
4. Promotion and publicity abroad.
5. Overseas training of personnel.
6. Extra expenditure on imports resulting from consumption by residents who have earned income from the tourist industry or whose consumption patterns have altered due to the demonstration effects of tourism.

Not surprisingly, these costs are not very well documented in the literature. Recent figures from New Zealand suggest that the overseas content in the construction of a 100–200 room hotel is in the order of 8–12 per cent (Tourism Advisory Council (TAC), 1978). The import content of tourist expenditure of visitors staying at first class hotels in Guatemala has been estimated at 23 per cent compared with 26 per cent for the most important manufacturing industry (foodstuffs). For cheaper hotels, the import content was much less (Schawinski cited by Theuns, 1976).

A similar approach to this can also be adopted for assessing the role of tourism in regional and local economies. A study of Eastbourne guest houses, for example, showed that first round leakages from that sector amounted to £17 for every £100 of income, but that ultimately only half the original sum was retained in the town (English Tourist Board, 1977). The comparatively low initial leakage indicates a very high degree of local ownership and employment.

The extent of these leakages and the degree to which goods and services consumed by foreign or extra-regional tourists can be provided domestically can vary enormously and will depend on (IUOTO, 1975; Theuns, 1976):

(a) the structure and diversity of the national or regional economy;
(b) the size of the nation;
(c) whether or not supply can keep pace with demand;
(d) the siting of development – remote areas may draw more on imported goods due to the uncertainty of domestic supplies;
(e) the class of visitor (see Table 4.3);
(f) the nation's import policy – the import content in Yugoslavia's tourist industry is as low as 2 per cent.

The extent of these leakages will also depend heavily on the development process (Ch. 2). Relatively more benefits will accrue to the host population with catalytic rather than integrated development. Leakages in peripheral destinations may be extremely high as a result of the structures and relationships depicted in Fig. 2.5.

Employment

As a service industry it is generally argued that tourism is labour intensive and that the principal type of labour demanded is semi-skilled or unskilled. As it is precisely that type of labour which is in abundant supply in most developing countries or depressed regions, then tourism's contribution to creating jobs or reducing unemployment can be significant. However, much tourism employment is seasonal or part-time in nature. Depending on the circumstances, for example, the seasonality of other activities, this may be an advantage or a drawback. Care must therefore be taken in assessing employment figures. The effects of 100 permanent jobs is likely to be much different from those of 400 seasonal positions available for only three months of the year, even though the two situations may offer the same number of full-time job equivalents.

Assessment of tourism's real contribution to employment generation is also rendered difficult by the diversity of the industry. Many studies to date have concentrated on the accommodation sector alone. In many cases this is to underestimate seriously the situation as Table 4.7 indicates. The hotel, restaurant and entertainment sector in these French ski resorts is shown to account for well under half of all employment. This is largely due to the recreational orientation of this type of tourism and the reduced role of hotels in these resorts (see Ch. 2). Although such a breakdown can be obtained from surveys, at a national or

Table 4.7 Distribution of employment in integrated ski resorts in France – 1975–76 (in %) (Knafou, 1978, p. 141)

RESORT	PUBLIC SERVICES	LIFTS, TRAILS	SKI SCHOOL	SHOPS
Avoriaz	2.6	31.2	7.7	12.8
Flaine	2.2	14.2	8.5	8.7
Isola 2000	10.2	20.1	13	5.6
La Plagne†	1.9	12.4	7.7	16.6

* Includes tourist office, sports club, heating, ice rink
† 1974–75
N.C. Not Counted

regional level the only distinct tourism category in official statistics may be the hotel, restaurant and cafe sector. Even that may include a fair degree of non-tourist use.

Noting such difficulties, Haughton *et al.* (1975) have estimated that in any EEC country, employment in the hotel and catering sector constitutes over 2.5 per cent of the total labour force. Although this proportion may seem relatively small, when the secondary effects of international and domestic tourist spending are included, these writers suggest that a total of 8½ – 10 million jobs would be lost in the event of the total withdrawal of the tourist industry. The proportion of total employment attributable to tourism was thought to vary from about 5 per cent in Belgium to over 9 per cent in France, Germany and Italy. These national figures may conceal significant local or regional variations in tourist employment. The Tayside study (Henderson, 1975), showed that while tourism spending created only about 4 per cent of total employment for the region as a whole, for Highland centres such as Pitlochry this figure rose to as high as 33 per cent.

As was noted earlier, the number of jobs created in Tayside depended on the type of accommodation developed. Where labour costs are high, as in many resorts of Western Europe, both developers and tourists are increasingly favouring accommodation with a low labour content such as rental apartments and condominiums.

Regional development

Tourism has been traditionally seen as an important tool for regional development. Early writers such as Selke (1936) and Christaller (1954, 1964) stressed that tourism tends to develop on the periphery and may thus stimulate economic activity in outlying regions or peripheral countries. Christaller went so far as to characterize tourism as being one activity which avoids central places. Clearly this is not the case with all types of tourism, as evidenced by the significance of tourism in London, Paris and Tokyo. Moreover, these early studies tended to neglect the leakages from these peripheral economies. These may be larger than elsewhere and developmental costs may be greater than in already established areas (Bryden, 1973). This notwithstanding, areas not attractive to other activities such as manufacturing or agriculture – for example, alpine areas, rocky coasts or coral atolls – may offer a viable base for tourist development. Such areas cannot usually compete with urbanized lowland regions for manufacturing but may offer a competitive advantage as far as tourism is concerned, especially in so far as many types of industrial development are incompatible with tourism and the two areas may complement each other. Given tourism's employment-generating potential, tourist development may thus act as an effective means for redressing regional disparities.

HOTELS, RESTAURANTS, ENTERTAINMENT	HEALTH	OTHERS*	CONSTRUCTION
36.8	1.2	7.7	N.C.
45.3	0.8	7.2	13.1
47.4	1.2	2.5	N.C.
42.3	1.5	10.3	9.3

The evidence from the literature is far from clear cut. Tourism is shown to both alleviate and accentuate regional economic imbalances. Both effects are evident in the Canaries (Odouard, 1973). Concentration of tourism in Las Palmas has extended the influence of that city on the island of Grande Canarie. In Tenerife, on the other hand, the more even dispersal of tourist activity has limited the growth of the capital, Santa Cruz. Peppelenbosch and Tempelman (1973) observe that in developing countries the most attractive regions are often developed so rapidly that balanced regional development is scarcely possible and that regional contrasts may in fact be heightened by 'over-developed' tourist areas, as in the case of the island of Djerba in southern Tunisia.

In such regions tourism has often developed spontaneously. Elsewhere, tourism has been consciously used as a regional development tool. France, for example, has major tourist development plans for Languedoc-Roussillon, Aquitaine, Corsica and the Alps. Regional development objectives have also been important in planning for tourism in Scotland and Mexico. Pacific decision-makers are now facing the question of whether tourism is a viable strategy for developing 'outer islands', that is, islands peripheral to the main centres of population.

The multiplier effect

Much discussion of tourism's contribution to regional development, and to economic development in general, concerns the way in which tourist spending filters throughout the economy, stimulating other sectors as it does so. This is the so-called 'tourist multiplier' effect. It should be remembered at the outset, however, that the 'tourist multiplier' is but a modification of a standard Keynesian multiplier which was first developed in a general context in the 1930s. This multiplier effect is not confined solely to tourism as some studies seem to imply. What is at question is whether the multiplier effect of tourism is any greater or lesser than that of industry, forestry or agriculture.

Initially, some impressive claims were put forward for tourism. Multipliers in the order of 3.2–4.3 for the Pacific (Clement, 1961) and 2.3 for the Caribbean (Zinder, 1969), were later considered exaggerated by other writers (Bryden, 1973) who have advanced much lower figures (0.55–0.85). Much of the confusion in the literature arises out of the use of different methodologies, the failure to recognize that different types of multipliers exist, that scale is important (leakages will be larger out of local rather than national economies) and that different economic contexts will give different results (diverse, integrated economies will result in larger multipliers). The basic types of multipliers will be briefly outlined here but for a more technical discussion of these the reader is referred to Archer (1977).

Sales or output multiplier. This measures the total sales or output induced in the economy from the initial expenditure and is expressed as a ratio of these. Thus, if $100 spent by a hotel guest results in second round spending of $50 as the hotel waitress spends her wages on a new dress and a further $25 of sales is made in a third round as the boutique owner buys her weekly meat and groceries then a total of $175 of sales results from the hotel guest's initial $100. This would give a sales multiplier of 1.75 after three rounds of spending. Sales multipliers are generally larger than other types of multipliers. They should not be confused with the income multiplier.

Income multiplier. This shows the relationship between tourist spending and changes in income and is generally calculated by the use of an *ad hoc* multiplier using the formula:

$$K = A \times \frac{1}{1-BC} \quad \text{where:}$$

A = Per cent of tourist spending remaining in the region after first round leakages,

B = Per cent of income of local residents spent on local goods and services,

C = Per cent of expenditure of local residents that accrues as local income, i.e. minus other leakages.

Thus, if 50 per cent of tourist spending remains after first-round leakages and if residents spend 60 per cent of their incomes locally and 40 per cent of that accrues as local income then the income multiplier is $0.5 \times \dfrac{1}{1 - 0.6 \times 0.4}$ or 0.65.

Employment multiplier   The employment multiplier describes the ratio of direct and secondary employment generated by additional employment to direct employment alone. Thus, if 100 new jobs created in the tourist industry gave rise to a further twenty jobs in supporting industries, then the employment multiplier would be 120/100 or 1.2. A second form of employment multiplier relates the amount of employment created by a given unit of tourism expenditure, for example, the total number of new jobs generated by, say, $10,000 of tourist spending.

When using multipliers or reading the literature other considerations must also be kept in mind. The propensity to consume is likely to be the same for all sectors of a given economy, given comparable levels of income. As a result, the most useful focus may be on 'leakages' especially between different types of tourist development. In general, the overall multiplier effects for the economy may be expected to differ more from country to country than for various sectors of a particular economy (IUOTO, 1975). Moreover, the multiplier effect of tourism or of particular types of tourist development must not be considered alone but in conjunction with other factors including: the capital/output ratio, the investment/employment ratio, foreign exchange earnings, growth rates and demand. Finally, on a practical level, detailed data are required for the various formulae to be calculated accurately. This writer has occasionally encountered a marked reluctance by tourist operators to impart even the most basic figures on sales or expenses. Other writers, notably Archer (1973) and Henderson (1975), appear to have been much more successful. Their studies suggest one of the most useful applications of tourist multipliers may be at the local or regional level when considering the differing forms of development to foster (see Table 4.8).

Table 4.8   Tourist sales and income multipliers in Anglesey, 1970.

CATEGORY OF TOURIST	MULTIPLIER	
(by type of accommodation)	Sales	Income
Hotel	1.4488	0.3063
Farmhouse and bed and breakfast	1.1959	0.7614
Caravan	0.8761	0.2171
Tent	1.4717	0.3097
Composite effect	1.0775	0.3260

Source: Archer, 1973, p. 57.

To date, multiplier studies and other forms of economic analysis, for example, input-output studies, have not greatly clarified tourism's capability as an economic stimulus *vis à vis* other sectors of the economy. What does emerge is that the effect of tourist spending is usually greater on employment than on income generation. Archer (1973) found in Anglesey, for example, that an extra £10,000 of general spending generated 2.39 jobs compared with 4.83 jobs for £10,000 of tourist spending, whereas the income effect of the two types of expenditure was approximately the same.

Inter-sectoral competition

Although tourism may stimulate other sectors of the economy, it may also disrupt or compete with them, especially where there is a shortage of labour or investment capital. Some relationships between tourism and agriculture illustrate these points well. A particularly striking case is that given by Long (1978), of the development of tourism in the British Virgin Islands. This led to a massive increase in GNP but the impact on agriculture was less satisfactory. The demand for agricultural imports increased from $1.8 m in 1969 to $4.3 m in 1974 and there was a significant decline in national agricultural output. This was attributed to a redeployment of the bulk of farm labour in the tourism sector, the displacement of local products by competition from North American ones and banks giving credit to businessmen rather than farmers. Elsewhere, however, tourism, by creating a demand for labour and stimulating rural depopulation, may effectively lead to a modernization of agricultural production (Boaglio, 1973). A more widespread effect is the inflation of land prices which may result in structural problems for agriculture (Guermond, 1974).

Inflation

The development of tourism may also have a general inflationary effect, especially during the initial stages when the supply of goods and services can often not respond quickly enough to meet the increased demand. Moreover, there is often a significant disparity between the spending power of the tourists and the host population. Housing prices in particular may rise very quickly, with tourists seeking holiday homes and external developers and employees looking for rental or permanent accommodation. Seasonal fluctuations in the price of food are often exacerbated by tourism.

State revenues

The main State benefits to be derived from tourist development will result from greater tax revenues (income, corporate, sales, property), increased overseas earnings, reduced social charges (e.g. unemployment benefits) and perhaps profits from direct intervention in the industry (e.g. State hotel chains). In Ireland it has been calculated that an increase of £10 million in gross tourist receipts, applying the multiplier principle, means an extra £5 million in tax revenue (OECD, 1967). These benefits will be reduced by the charges incurred in developing the industry, such as investment in infrastructure, development incentives and promotional and training expenses. The infrastructure charges may be especially onerous for local authorities as this sector should be developed at the outset, requires reasonably large amounts of capital, brings little or no direct income and indirect returns in the form of taxes or rates are largely in the long term. New and heavy operating expenses may also be borne by the local authorities, for example, rubbish disposal and road maintenance, especially snow clearance in ski resorts.

Who benefits? Who pays?

Finally, in assessing these various costs and benefits, it is important throughout to identify just what groups or individuals are being affected. Four broad groups may be identified. Firstly there are those directly involved in the development process – the promoters, operators and their employees. Much of the direct return from tourism will accrue to this group. Then there are the other residents and enterprises who may not be directly engaged in any tourist activity but whose lives may nevertheless be affected by the expansion of tourism. Many of the indirect costs, such as the diversion of capital, land and labour and tourist-induced inflation, may be felt by this sector of the community, although benefits may be experienced as well. The public authorities may be development agents, as was noted in Chapter 2, but it is useful to distinguish them from the private sector in that the nature of their benefits and costs may differ significantly from those of the private sector. Finally, in paying for the various services they demand and use, the tourists bear many of the direct costs. Their benefits tend to be essentially non-monetary ones. Where, however, the advent of international tourism pushes up prices, extra charges may be incurred by the domestic holidaymaker.

When the geographic origin of each of these four groups (Fig. 4.2) is considered along with their internal diversity, then very complex situations may exist. However, the point can be made with a simpler case, that of Brighton. Commenting on the 'two faces' of the town, Gray and Lowerson (1979) observe: 'Externally generated wealth remains of great importance, but much of it has been ploughed into projects whose value does little for the chronic problems of the town, particularly an inadequately housed low-wage labour force competing for resources with visitors and growing number of students.'

CONCLUSIONS

Clearly no simple statement can be made regarding the impact of tourist development other than that its effects may be very diverse and far-reaching and that they will vary from case to case according to the context and the process of development. Tables 4.1, 4.5 and 4.7 attempt to provide suitable frameworks for studying particular types of impact. Many specific assessment techniques, however, require further development and refinement. But, following Table 4.1, perhaps the greatest need is for improved methods of assessing the overall impact of tourist development by weighing economic costs and benefits expressed essentially in quantitative terms against social and environmental gains and losses, many of which can only be expressed qualitatively. Finally, beyond these considerations lies the critical question of decision-making. Even if the degree of impact can be accurately established, who is to decide what levels are desirable or acceptable?

CHAPTER 5
SPATIAL PLANNING FOR TOURISM

INTRODUCTION

In Chapter 2, tourism was shown to be a diffuse and rather complex activity, consisting as it does of a wide range of elements which may be developed by a broad spectrum of developers, having different aspirations and capabilities. Chapter 4 showed tourist development touches not only the tourists and developers but also other sectors of society, the economy in general and the environment as a whole. In particular, problems arise and costs are increased when the different sectors of the industry do not develop harmoniously or when the motives and capabilities of the different development agents conflict. Carried to an extreme, uncontrolled growth of tourism can irrevocably destroy the very resource base on which it was built. Because of these factors, the ECE (1976, p. 8) concluded that: 'the growth of the tourist industry cannot be left to follow demand forces alone'. Some degree of planning is necessary to co-ordinate and synchronize the development of the different sectors, to balance competing and sometimes conflicting claims on the same limited resource base, to maximize the positive impacts of tourist development and to minimize its adverse effects. In the long run, directive measures will usually prove less expensive than corrective ones.

In general, tourism planning should seek to co-ordinate the different sectors outlined earlier in terms of their development in time and through space with regard to market demand and specified objectives. Such co-ordination should also be extended to linkages with other economic and social activities. The roles of the different development agents, particularly those of the public and private sectors, should be defined so as to avoid unnecessary competition, duplication of some tasks and the neglect of others. Such a definition should take into account the financial and technical competence of the different development agents. More specific measures will depend on the particular objectives of the development programme and on the level of planning.

Varying goals and objectives for tourist development can be defined. These must be formulated at an early stage of the planning process, although some initial research into markets and the existing state of the industry will be required. National objectives of tourism planning in Scotland centre on improving the balance of payments and increasing the social benefits from holiday taking (Carter, 1977). Regional objectives include raising incomes and creating employment in rural regions, providing social infrastructure and conservation of the environment. Although economic objectives remain important in highly developed and urbanized countries, growing emphasis is being placed on social and environmental goals. Planners in West Germany (Klopper, 1976) and Switzerland (Keller, 1976), for instance, stress the need to provide recreational facilities for their urban populations and to protect the environment. Other more specific tourist industry objectives may be defined amongst general, social and economic goals. Objectives of the Greek Tourist Plan (1978–82) include the overcoming of seasonal constraints and the balancing of hotels with other types of accommodation (Kalogérepoulou and Rozolis, 1978). Certain general economic goals are also translated into numeric targets, such as increasing tourist receipts annually by 19 per cent to reach 2,340 million dollars by 1982.

Planning cannot be done in a vacuum and national or regional goals must be translated into geographic terms. Commenting on tourism planning in Turkey, Ersek and Duzgunoglu (1976, p. 69) note:

> Significant problems in this field have been encountered during the implementation stages of the First Five-Year Plan and during the first two years of the Second Plan (1963–72) due to lack of policy decisions and tools to indicate the spatial distribution of resources and priority areas.
>
> The definition of priority areas and policy decisions concerning the geographical distribution of resources is of prime importance for a country like Turkey. This is especially so because of the scale and variety of Turkey's tourism resources.

Similar sentiments were expressed a decade earlier by the president of the New Zealand Travel and Holidays Association (NZTHA, 1966, p. 1):

> Queenstown is desperate for additional first class accommodation and at the Hermitage there is scarcely a single outdoor tourist amenity except the ski-planes. Yet an ice-skating rink has been opened at Queenstown and a new block of bedrooms approved for the Hermitage. Both these places may warrant such developments, but an overall plan would surely put first things first . . . a plan must be devised, to properly balance and regulate expenditure and development on such things as tourist hotels, national parks, dispersal hotels, tourist roads, internal transport and all those things that go to make a composite tourist industry.

These two comments highlight the need for a geographical perspective in planning at a national level. It will be extremely unlikely that any country will have the resources to develop all its tourist possibilities simultaneously. Consequently, priority areas must be defined. Care in the selection and development of these areas is essential, given the number of factors which may influence tourist development (Ch. 3) and the composite nature of the industry (Ch. 2). Moreover, once developed, the tourism product is fixed in space and cannot be transferred easily.

This chapter concentrates on these spatial aspects of tourism planning as there has been little attempt in the literature on tourism to review systematically this important field of planning. Moreover, it is in this field that applied geographers are most likely to make their contribution to the planning process. For further information on other specialized aspects, such as marketing, economic planning and the more technical aspects of physical planning, the reader is referred to more specific works such as those by Wahab et al. (1976), Gearing et al. (1976) and Lawson and Baud-Bovy (1977), as well as general texts on tourism planning (Kaiser and Helber, 1978; Gunn, 1979).

The concerns and emphases of spatial planning vary at different levels. At a national and regional level particular consideration will be given to the selection and distribution of areas to be developed. Account will be taken not only of tourist potential but also the economic, social and environmental objectives of development as well as relationships with other sectors of the economy. At the level of the individual town or resort, greater attention will be given to actual physical lay-out and structure. National planning is considered first, followed by planning at the regional then local levels. Much of the literature concerns local planning as there is a greater number and a wider variety of examples at this scale. There is as yet little evidence of spatial planning at an international level although various regional tourist associations such as the Pacific Area Travel Association (PATA) do exist.

PLANNING AT THE NATIONAL LEVEL

A major concern at the national level is to determine the most important regions to develop (UN, 1970). For those nations with an as yet poorly developed tourist industry, this will involve an examination of the country's tourist resources along the lines discussed in Chapter 3, and the delimitation of one or several areas to develop. In other nations where tourism is already a significant activity it may be a question of where or how to concentrate future growth. Elsewhere, the prime concern may be to identify and rectify bottle-necks and deficiencies in the national tourist system rather than to promote new areas. This is especially important in countries such as New Zealand where the emphasis, for overseas visitors at least, is on touring rather than destination-orientated tourism. Bottle-necks in one or two key places may effectively limit the growth of tourism throughout the country as a whole.

In all cases, selection of areas should be guided by national planning objectives. In Mexico, for example, specific planning criteria have been defined (Collins, 1979, p. 354): 'New tourist centres should develop new sources of employment in areas with tourist potential. These areas should be located near important rural centres with low incomes and few alternatives to develop other productive activities in the near future. New resorts should spur regional development with new agricultural, industrial and handicraft activities in the zones.' These and other factors led to the development of Mexico's first planned tourism complex in economically depressed Quintana Roo (Cancun) in preference to other more developed areas such as Acapulco, or equally depressed regions like the Coast of Oaxaca which, however, lack infrastructure.

One of the objectives of Thai national planning has been to foster growth selectively throughout the country by designating key development areas (see below). In Bali, on the other hand, to limit some of the socially disruptive effects of tourism, planners have attempted to confine development to Kuta, Sanur and Denpasar (Cohen, 1978).

Spatial co-ordination with other sectors of the economy is also important at the national level. Development of major infrastructure such as roads, airports or ports, for example, should take into account not only the needs and demands of tourism but also those of other sectors such as agriculture or manufacturing. Such co-ordination is also necessary to ensure that valuable tourist resources are not destroyed by other activities. Campagnoli-Ciaccio (1975), for instance, observes how the tourist development of much of the Sicilian coastline was seriously compromised by the installation of large oil refineries.

Structurally, one of the major concerns at a national level will be linking development areas with gateway cities. In many countries the majority of arrivals by air will be to a single city, and links with the hinterland, particularly in developing countries, may not be strong. Even in economically advanced countries where such linkages exist, for example, Japan and the United Kingdom, international tourists may still be heavily concentrated in the capital city (Tokyo receives two thirds of the bed nights spent by the international tourists in Japan). Selective development of a small number of key tourist regions will reduce the number of linkages to be developed and at the same time permit the promotion of a stronger, more coherent image of these regions enabling them to compete more effectively with the points of arrival. However, in large countries where the potential is for touring rather than resort development, promotion of a second major entry/exit point will help increase the flow of visitors throughout the country and obviate the need for them to backtrack. But where the concern is for social tourism and promoting the recreational opportunities of nationals, the emphasis will be towards developing more localized linkages between the major urban areas and their immediate hinterlands.

In most cases, development of domestic tourism and international tourism will be complementary. The Dubrovnik Seminar (UN, 1970) noted:

> in some countries development of domestic tourism might lead to a development of foreign tourism, whilst in others, as yet undeveloped, but well endowed with tourist attractions, the encouragement of foreign tourism would lead in due course to growth in domestic tourism. In both cases, however, tourist development plans should provide from the start for both foreign and domestic tourists.

A number of national tourist development plans have been prepared in recent years, particularly in developing countries: Thailand's National Plan on Tourism Development (TDC-SGV, 1976), Philippines' Ten-Year Development Plan of the Department of Tourism (1977–86), the Grenada Tourism Development Plan (OAS, 1978), Egypt's National Tourism Plan (Elmasri et al., 1978) and Israel's Master Plan for Tourism (Stock, 1977b). The Thai plan in particular is a good example of how spatial perspectives have been incorporated in a national plan and of how spatial planning relates to other aspects of the planning process.

National plan on tourism development — Thailand

Preparations for Thailand's National Plan on Tourist Development began in 1974 at the request of the Tourist Organization of Thailand. This followed a period of rapid growth in international tourism which saw the industry become the country's third largest source of overseas funds. The National Plan was to guide both government and private enterprise in meeting future growth by serving as a framework for feasibility studies and the development of master plans and detailed plans for selected tourism areas. The study was undertaken by an overseas consulting firm and a Thai one. The final report, on which this section is based, was published in 1976 (TDC-SGV, 1976).

Figure 5.1 outlines the basic study procedure. Analysis of demand and supply was accompanied by the formulation of objectives and guidelines for development. This in turn led to the identification of potential development areas, the formulation of a long-term development plan and the establishment of a development programme to 1980. Market analysis suggested a strong growth of international tourism which would give 2–2.5 million tourists by 1980. The majority of these, given the short length of stay (average duration of five days by 1980), would be spent in and around Bangkok. However, the demand for touring and cultural tourism would grow, necessitating the development of regional and district centres and an increase in leisure-orientated international travellers would give rise to resort development. A strong growth in domestic tourism was also foreseen, but, given income levels, this would mainly involve day-trips and, to a lesser extent, weekend stays.

In terms of policies and guidelines, it was felt that product development should be market-orientated and the emphasis should be on unique Thai assets. Moreover (TDC-SGV, 1976, p. 3):

> Tourism facilities should be set up in such a way that they are suitable for integrated use by international and domestic tourists and recreation seekers of high, medium and

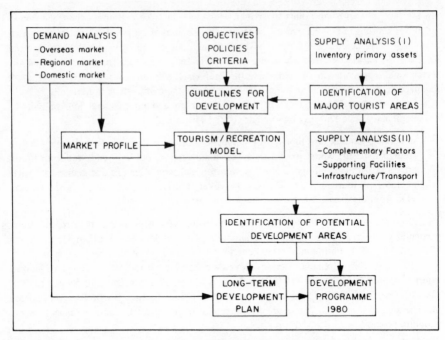

5.1 Study procedure for Thai National Plan on Tourism Development.
(TDC-SGV, 1976)

low income structure. To make the investments economically viable and to prevent disturbance of the traditional way of living, dispersed concentration of the facilities is imperative. Infrastructure and superstructure should be as much multipurpose as possible, serving also other sectors of the economy. Existing plant should be fully exploited and upgraded before new development is started. Strict regulations should control the environment.

The analysis of supply began with an inventory of the country's primary attractions. Some 510 attractions were identified, classified (by type and degree of importance) and plotted on a map. Subsequently sixteen major tourism areas were established using the following two major criteria:

1. Attractions have to lie within fairly short distances of each other.
2. These attractions need to have a high degree of quality and uniqueness.

These sixteen areas were then weighted by other criteria to establish development priorities (Table 5.1). In particular, with respect to the national tourism/recreation model, importance was attached to accessibility and pressure from urban areas.

Within these sixteen areas, a hierarchy of twenty-one tourist centres was then selected for long-term development. Three are to be developed as regional centres (1st echelon), ten as district centres (six, 2nd echelon; four 3rd echelon), and eight as resorts (4th echelon). In addition, twelve major towns with over 20,000 inhabitants were designated as tourism support centres in the overall tourism network (three, 4th echelon; nine, 5th echelon), only three of these being within major tourism areas. In the plan, Bangkok/Pattaya continues to be dominant but the other two regional centres of Chiang Mai and Songkhla/Hat Yai are to become the nuclei for tourist development in the North

Table 5.1 Evaluation of potential tourism development areas in Thailand (*National Plan on Tourism Development*)

(1) MAJOR TOURISM AREAS	(2) PRIMARY ATTRACTIONS	(3) COMPLEMENTARY FACTORS	(4) SUPPORTING FACILITIES	(5) ACCESSIBILITY*	(6) URBAN RECREATION PRESSURE	(7) TOURISM PRESSURE	(8) SCORE
Bangkok/Pattaya	+++	+	+++	++++	+++	+++	17
Chiang Mai	++	+++	++	++++	++	++	14
Songkhla/Hat Yai	++	++	++	+++	++	++	13
Phuket	+	+++	+	++	+	++	10
Hua Hin (Phetchaburi-Prachuap)	+	+	+	+	+	+	6
Kanchanaburi	+	++	0	+	+	+	6
Upper Central Region (Phitsanulok area)	++	+	0	++	+	+	6
Pattani/Narathiwat	++	0	0	++	+	+	5
Khorat	+	0	+	++	+	−	4
Ubon	+	0	+	+	+	+	4
Chanthaburi/Trat	+	+	+	0	0	+	4
Nakhon Si Thammarat	+	++	0	0	+	0	3
Chumphon	+	++	−	+	0	0	3
Trang/Phatthalung	+	+	−	+	+	0	2
Chiang Rai	++	+	0	0	0	0	2
Sakon Nakhon	+	+	0	0	0	−	1

* For column 5 only:
all modes of transport incl. international airport
all modes of transport incl. semi-international airport
domestic airport
railway access
highway access only

Score		
++++	4	very good/high
+++	3	good/high
++	2	fairly/moderate
+	1	poor/low
0	0	
−	−1	very poor/low

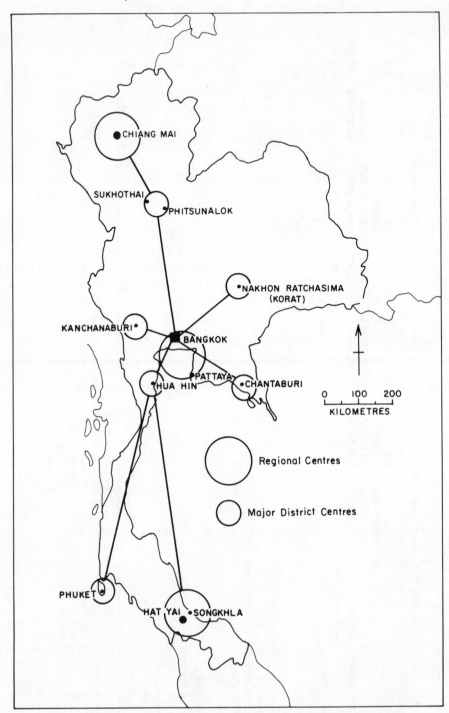

5.2 Recommended centres for short-term development in Thailand (1975–1980).
(TDC-SGV, 1976)

and South. Overseas tourists are expected to travel to these centres predominantly by air whereas domestic tourists will travel mainly overland. For the latter, intermediate centres will be important (district centres, country resorts and major towns).

The short-term programme (to 1980) aims therefore at immediate development of regional centres in the most attractive regions and of major district centres located within the network of regional centres (Fig. 5.2). Specific development measures for these are then outlined. The plan also recommends the strengthening of the Tourist Organization of Thailand by its conversion into a ministry which would co-ordinate the various government and semi-government organizations and guide and control the activities of the private sector. Major projects would be carried out by special agencies in which the private sector and the government would co-operate under the supervision of a Tourism Development Authority. Minor developments would be implemented at a lower level. Manpower requirements are also considered and the government is urged to provide more training courses at different levels.

Although sound in principle, it is too early yet to fully evaluate the Thai plan. By 1978, visitor arrivals had increased to 1,450,000, a 19 per cent increase over the previous year. If that rate of growth has continued, then the projected 1980 figures will have been attained, at least the lower estimate. The opening of an international air link from Chiang Mai to Hong Kong in 1980 will undoubtedly aid the distribution of some of these new tourists to the north.

PLANNING AT THE REGIONAL LEVEL

Tourist development regions will, in many cases, be defined by national plans although in other cases the initiative may come from the region. Tourist regions identified at the national level will usually be defined in terms of the spatial association of attractions and associated facilities, as in the Thai case (see also Ch. 3), or possibly in physical terms (a stretch of coast, a river system or a highland massif) or administrative ones, especially where tourism forms part of an overall regional strategy.

A first concern is with the choice of localities within the region which are to be developed. Some localities may have already been identified in the initial selection process but frequently more specific site evaluation will be required using the methods discussed in Chapter 3. At the same time, the regional objectives must be kept in mind, together with structural considerations. Where the aim is to limit social impact only one or two centres may be developed – the 'dispersed concentration' of the Thai plan – but where growth is to be spread throughout the region a larger number of development centres may be established. Economic and social objectives may also determine the choice between developing new functional 'ex-nihilo' in virgin areas or grafting new tourist activities on to the existing settlement pattern, though this choice will also depend of course on the extent of existing development. In general, the degree of local participation and regional stimulus will be increased where existing settlements are incorporated into the development plan (see Ch. 2).

Some form of structural hierarchy will usually be necessary. A major regional centre may serve as a gateway to the region, provide many of the higher order services and functions, project a stronger promotional image and generally act as a development pole. Such a centre might be developed around the greatest concentration of attractions or a major settlement but some completely new base resort might also be created, as with La Plagne in the La Grande Plagne complex. Although a range of facilities might be offered in the regional centre, smaller centres might specialize in providing particular services or

5.3 Aquitaine tourist development plan.
(After la Documentation Française, *L'Aménagement de la Côte Aquitaine*, 1971, p. 30)

serving specific sectors of the market (e.g. families, the elderly, the sports-minded). The staged development of these centres may also allow for a more ready adaptation to changes in market demand.

The transport network, which plays the essential role of linking these various centres together, may also be hierarchical. In the cases of the coastal regions of Languedoc-Roussillon and Aquitaine, regional motorways run the length of the region, linking development units to each other and the region to the country as a whole (Fig. 5.3 and 6.3). Expressways connect the principal resorts to the regional motorway and smaller roads carry sight-seeing traffic and cross protected areas. Where the motorways are located some distance inland, instead of following the coast, a hierarchical transport network can serve as a major environmental tool by relieving pressure on certain fragile areas (Fig. 5.4).

Environmental considerations become important at the regional level where a range of spatial strategies may be implemented. Zoning measures may encourage the concentration or dispersion of tourist activity. The concentration option favours the location of all or most facilities in certain designated localities, preferably highly resistant environments as determined by studies of carrying capacity. Conversely, the dispersion policy encourages the distribution of smaller scale developments throughout the region, so as to reduce the environmental pressures on any particular spot. Concentration has been favoured in some coastal regions where a prime objective has been to avoid ribbon development the complete length of the coastline. In virgin areas such a policy may be reinforced by economic considerations; for example, the costs of providing infrastructure. A major concern in alpine areas is the altitude at which development should occur, with some writers favouring a move away from high altitude integrated resorts to development of accommodation at middle altitudes and linkages with the ski-fields (Chappis, 1974; Stanev, 1976). Areas to be left undeveloped, especially fragile areas, will need to be formally reserved by their designation as national or State parks, as some form of scenic or natural reserve, or by building codes. Dispersion may be more applicable to rural areas where facilities tend to be on a smaller scale. However, the uncontrolled dispersion of second homes can have unsightly results (Krippendorf, 1977).

A second technique is to relieve pressure on fragile areas by encouraging development elsewhere or by redirecting the tourist traffic. The impact on the coast may be reduced by measures to develop tourism in depth, that is, by distributing growth further inland. This may also spread the economic benefits. Or, access may be given to another forest or a second ski-field may be developed to reduce demand on areas reaching saturation. This is the so-called 'honey-pot' strategy which may be particularly effective if the new attraction intercepts traffic heading from the city to a pressure point. Krippendorf (1977) also suggests improving conditions within the city, so as to reduce the need to escape the urban environment, thus reducing demand on surrounding areas at its very source.

Several of these strategies have been incorporated into the plan to develop the Aquitaine coastline. This is a sandy stretch of coastline, some 250 km long. The coast is backed by the extensive pine forest of the Landes, amidst which is located a chain of small lakes. Parts of this environment are fragile and unstable. There is but a thin soil layer in the forest, thus the effects of trampling by large numbers of visitors could be quite disastrous. The effects of trampling on the coastal dunes could also be serious, for any blow-out would expose the forest to the burning effects of the salt-laden sea breezes. Moreover the forests could be suffocated by the invasion of the sand. Figure 5.3 shows the coast has been divided into seventeen sectors – nine development units (125,000 hectares) and eight protected areas (265,000 hectares). Moreover, each development unit is to

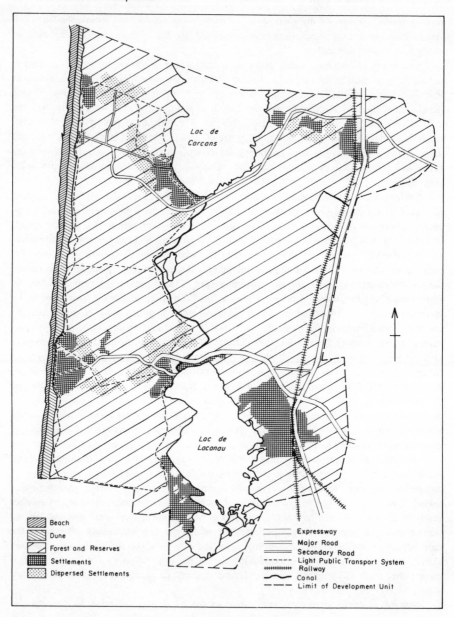

5.4 Tourist Development Unit 3 – Aquitaine.
(After Mission Interministérielle pour l'Aménagement Touristique de la Côte Aquitaine, *Schéma d'Aménagement Touristique de la Côte Aquitaine, mars 1972*)

be developed in depth. Such a policy is assisted by a more favourable micro-climate in the forest and by the existence of an alternative to the coastal beaches in the form of the small lakes located 10–20 km inland. This has enabled a development perpendicular to the coast, whereby traditional coastal resorts have been complemented by small-scale sub-divisions in the forest and other developments on the lake shores (Fig. 5.4).

Other regional planning considerations are examined more comprehensively with reference to Languedoc-Roussillon in the following chapter.

PLANNING AT THE LOCAL LEVEL

Much spatial planning at the local level concerns the physical organization of the sectors outlined in Chapter 2. The primary attractions, be they natural or historical, will commonly be a focus for planning as their location is often fixed and their features vulnerable. The distinction between transport to and within the destination is critical at this level. The range of accommodation types, including residential housing, must be kept in mind and appropriate densities and height limitations determined. Provision must be made for services such as shops and restaurants as well as other functions and forms of land use, particularly where tourism is but one of several activities. Development will take several forms depending on whether planning is for a beach resort, an historic or cultural centre, or for tourism in an urban area. Details and emphasis will also vary from site to site but several general principles and considerations apply to most situations.

A first concern is not to compromise the site, either physically or visually, by the injudicious location of buildings or other facilities. Coastal sites may be particularly vulnerable. Development on or removal of the foredune, for example, can present serious erosion problems. Obtrusive sitings listed by the An Foras Forbartha (1970) report on amenity and tourism planning in Ireland include those on a ridge or hilltop, those breaking the waterline or not considering existing hedgerow patterns. Conversely, unobtrusive sitings include those against a backdrop of trees, hills or those taking advantage of existing landscape features. Other examples of integrative planning are given by the ICSID Interdesign Seminar (Gorman et al., 1977) and Lawson and Baud-Bovy (1977). Coupled with this is the more general need to develop the area harmoniously. This implies an adequate balance between and within the different sectors in terms of capacity, quality and style as well as compatibility of different functions. Klopper (1976), for example, notes the need for liveliness in some parts of spas and silence and cure facilities in others. Compatibility with non-tourist activities is also a major consideration. The design of the resort should be such that as many people as possible have ready access to the attractions and facilities. At the same time it must be recognized that different forms of accommodation are able to support different land prices or rents. In general, the more intensive the form, the higher the prices that can be paid. For instance, hotels will usually support higher prices than motels, and blocks of apartments more expensive sites than villas. Land prices will reflect the characteristics of the site and its location. Prime sites will be those with a better outlook and environment and will generally be located closer to the main attractions, though isolation may be a feature of some quality developments. Careful design, however, particularly of street lay-out, should still allow general freedom of access from most parts of the resort or centre to the main areas of recreational activity or tourist interest. Finally, the constraints of the site must be taken into account. In many coastal, alpine or other natural areas, only certain limited zones may be built upon due to soil or slope stability, the suitability of geological structures or drainage conditions. In historic or urban areas these constraints may arise more from the existing pattern of land use.

Some of the specific characteristics of coastal resorts, urban centres and historic towns will now be examined in more detail.

Coastal resorts

Coastal resorts are perhaps the most common and distinctive form of tourist development, the coast being the premier tourist destination in many countries. Much of their distinctiveness arises from their location along the beach or seashore. For as Stansfield (1969) points out, growth outwards from a central core is limited to approximately only 180° as opposed to a full 360° in most other urban areas. Many of the older beach resorts, whether in England, France or the United States, have developed spontaneously along the traditional beach front or 'front de mer' (Gilbert 1939, 1945; Burnet, 1963; Barret cited by Wall, 1971; Stansfield, 1969). Typically, this consists of a parallel association of the beach, a promenade (or the boardwalk in the United States), a road or highway and a first line of accommodation and commerce where the best hotels and most expensive shops and apartments are to be found along with the casino. Beyond this, the intensity of accommodation decreases. This parallel structure now presents several disadvantages (Pearce, 1978c). Firstly, the first line of buildings, which are often high-rise in order to support the higher land prices, may constitute a barrier, both visual and real, between the interior residential zones and the beach or port. Secondly, the flow of pedestrians from these zones to the beach is disrupted by the automobile traffic of the intervening road, particularly if this happens to be a regional highway. Moreover, such a structure encourages linear or ribbon development, which is often not only aesthetically displeasing but also environmentally degrading, especially where continuous stretches of the coastline are developed. Resorts developed more recently in France exhibit a number of innovations and a greater degree of co-ordination. The solutions adopted by the newer resorts depend on their size and particular orientation.

The growing popularity of yachting and recreational boating in France since the 1960s has led to the development of specialized coastal resorts where the port is no longer a mere adjunct to the beach resort, but the very heart of the development. Port Grimaud, situated on the Mediterranean coastline in the Gulf of St Tropez, was developed by the architect F. Spoerry, whose basic idea was to bring together man, his home and his boat by the inter-penetration of the sea and dwellings. This was achieved by the development of small islands and inter-connecting canals on formerly waste marshland (Fig. 5.5). The idea itself is not so new, for in many respects, including some of the architecture, Port Grimaud is a replica in miniature of Venice. What is innovative is the adaptation of this form for purely recreational purposes. The borders of each island have been developed as quaysides and mooring berths have been installed. As the dwellings themselves have been constructed virtually on the water's edge this enables each holiday-maker to literally step out the back door on to his boat or yacht. Essentially a parallel structure has been retained – canal, berth, footway, accommodation and vehicle access – but this has been so designed as to create a very functional resort with an accompanying holiday ambience throughout. The system of islands also assures a much greater length of mooring space, and limitation of the buildings to two or three storeys maintains a balance between the number of accommodation units and mooring berths. Height limitations were also imposed by the nature of the foundations and were aesthetically desirable because of the low-lying environment. A car park at the entrance to the resort receives the cars of visitors who must continue on foot, and those of the residents who generally have vehicle access only to deliver their bags and goods. Consequently a calm atmosphere prevails with most of the movement by foot or canal, either by private boat or by means of an electrically-powered water bus.

The neighbouring Marines de Cogolin provides a different spatial expression of the same principle, the integration of the vacationer into his recreational environment, although the juxtaposition of accommodation and berths is less immediate than at Port

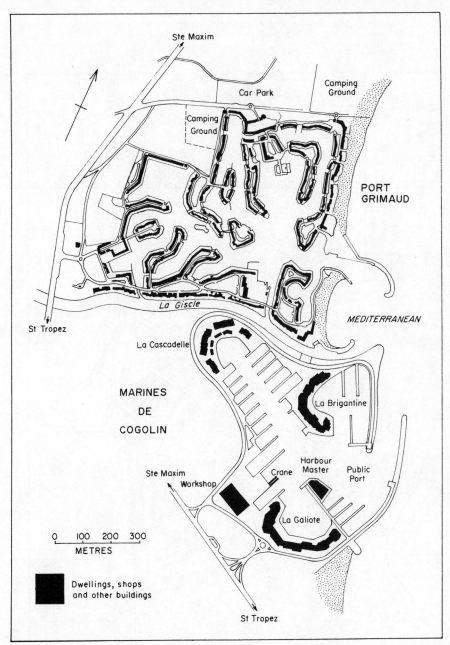

5.5 Port Grimaud and the Marines de Cogolin.

Grimaud. The Marines de Cogolin is comprised of three main basins, with a smaller public port reserved for passing boats at the harbour entrance (Fig. 5.5). The accommodation has been developed around each of the basins, rising in a series of steps so that the maximum number of residents enjoy a view of the port and the activities that take place

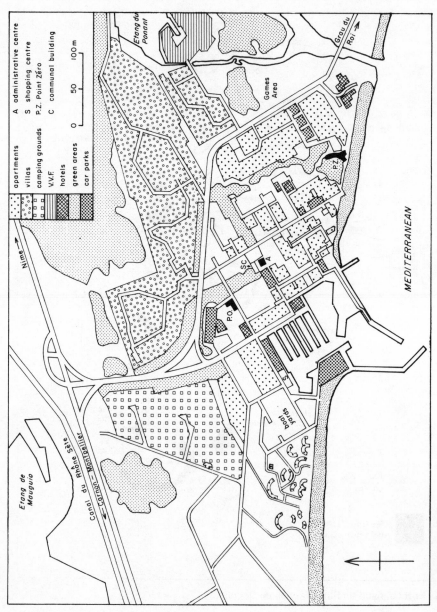

5.6 La Grande Motte.

there. This arena-like architecture is also more aesthetically appealing than the typical vertical high-rise buildings which would jar in this low-lying environment. Most of the shops are located on the ground floor of the Galiote which also houses a cinema and night club. While temporary access to the quayside is permitted for loading and unloading equipment and stores, the general vehicle traffic is restricted to the far side of the accommodation where parking is available either in garages at the rear of the dwellings which protect the vehicles from the salt-laden sea air or in public car parks. Thus largely undisturbed access by foot between dwelling and boat is again possible.

Other comparable developments include Port Camargue, near the mouth of Rhone, which, with a planned mooring space for 2,500 boats (one berth for less than five beds), is one of the largest recreational port complexes in Europe. Elsewhere smaller 'cités lacustres' form part of a larger or existing resort. At Port Barcares, the Cité Nautica serves as a sub-centre, focusing activity on the Etang de Barcares, whereas most of the resort looks out to sea. It must be remembered, however, that all these developments are along the Mediterranean, that is, in comparatively low energy situations. The extent of tidal movements in the Atlantic has limited such projects along France's western coastline, without excluding them entirely; for example, Port Deauville. Moreover, concern has been expressed regarding the 'privatization' of the seashore, and private developments built on the immediate seashore have now been restricted. Nevertheless, many of the principles still remain valid elsewhere, particularly the attempt to separate the different forms of traffic.

In larger resorts having activities other than boating, the port may be only one centre of activity and the principle of a single row of dwellings surrounding the harbour or stretching out along the beach is no longer valid. This is especially true if ribbon development is to be avoided and the resort given some depth. The beach and port will remain key elements in the structure of any seaside resort but the traditional 'front de mer' can be effectively modified as the new resorts along the Languedoc-Roussillon coastline have shown (see Ch. 6). La Grande Motte (43,000 beds) is one of the first and largest of these new resorts and embodies several new and interesting principles. A first concern at La Grande Motte has been to avoid some of the traffic and congestion problems inherent in the parallel structure of the traditional 'front de mer'. The major access road still parallels the sea but at a distance of 200 m or so from the beach (Fig. 5.6). Secondary roads terminating in car parks run perpendicular to this main road giving access to the beach. Such a 'comb' or 'glove' system removes traffic from the beach area while leaving it readily accessible from all parts of the resort. To further encourage pedestrians, landscaped footways have been developed and no part of La Grande Motte is more than 10 to 15 minutes by foot from the sea. As the densest accommodation is along the beach front, many of the residents live right on the beach itself. Point Zero provides a block of amenities for those using the eastern part of the beach. Overcrowding of the beach has been avoided as the amount of accommodation built has been a function of the beach's carrying capacity (see Ch. 3).

Although the average density at La Grande Motte is 100 beds per hectare, there is considerable variation in density within the resort itself (Fig. 5.6). The main access road cuts the resort in two. To the south, around the port and along the beach, are large, prestigious apartment buildings. Designed (by Jean Balladur) to ensure the maximum amount of insolation, these pyramid-shaped buildings give La Grande Motte its distinctive character and a general harmony of style although they have not been greeted with complete acceptance (Cazes, 1972). The ground floors of these pyramids are often occupied by shops and businesses, especially those around the port where many restaurants and terrace cafes are found. These multiple-unit dwellings become less dense and more conventional in form towards the interior of this zone, particularly to the east of the Avenue Melgueil where several buildings belonging to social organizations or housing more permanent workers are located. Few of the hotels have been able to locate on the most prestigious sites. The centre of the resort is comparatively empty, being occupied by gardens, a recreational arena and administrative buildings. Three distinct 'quartiers' are found to the north of the access road. Here a zone of individual houses and villas separates the camping grounds in the north-west from a family holiday camp (VVF) (Village Vacances Familiales), located on the shores of a secondary activity zone, the Etang du Ponant, which offers a range of water sports. More recently the area to the west of the port has been developed. Known as La Motte du Couchant, buildings there take a crescent-shaped form and tend to be lower lying than in the rest of the resort.

In the cases mentioned above new ideas and principles have been able to be incorporated freely. However, the renewal or expansion of older beach resorts is constrained by existing developments. In most cases the prime beach front sites have already been occupied. Thus it may be essential not only to renew existing developments, but to stimulate and concentrate further growth around a new centre of activity. Construction of ports or marinas has been successfully employed in Languedoc-Roussillon to give new life to existing resorts. At Carnon and St Cyprien, for example, new apartment blocks have been built around newly created ports. Although deprived of a view of the beach, the residents of these apartments enjoy the comings and goings of the port and so have a sense of participation in the life of the resort. Furthermore, through traffic at Carnon is gradually being diverted to a new highway at the interior of the resort and the present road forming part of the 'front de mer' will eventually be closed off to restore some tranquillity to the area. Access roads running perpendicular to the highway have opened a new zone of individual dwellings behind the band of existing beach front villas. As a result 7,000 new beds will be made available, more than doubling the existing capacity of Carnon.

Other problems have been experienced in the older coastal resorts. In Brighton, Gray and Lowerson (1979) note that planning attempts have been ambivalent. Measures to control the traffic and parking in the town centre have been offset by the encouragement of new traffic generators such as the marina and the conference trade. Conflict has arisen over the desire to protect historical façades and areas of scenic beauty and the demand for the development of much-needed low-cost housing.

Urban areas

As noted earlier, tourism may be very important in large cities and towns. Whether measured in terms of bed-nights or accommodation capacity, the level of tourist activity in many cities is higher than in those centres usually thought of as resorts. Cities may function as gateways or staging points but many will appeal in themselves, grouping, as they often do, a large range of historical or cultural attractions, recreational and entertainment facilities, shops and being a major object of business and conference travel. Many of these attractions and facilities are located in the city centre. Consequently, the centre has become the focus for the location of much accommodation as stays in urban areas are generally short and tourists want to see as much as possible in the time available to them. In this respect, the same locational forces that operate in resorts occur in cities. The planning situation differs, however, in that in the city tourism is but one of a number of competing land uses. Conflicts have arisen in many cases, the problem being exacerbated by the neglect of tourism by planning authorities or the multiplicity of agencies involved. In London, Eversley (1977) lists no fewer than eleven public bodies, each with its own particular concerns or policies regarding tourism.

A first step in many cases may thus be to recognize tourism as a particular form of land use, with its own characteristics and demands, and henceforth to incorporate it specifically in town or city plans. Direction of future tourist growth may both alleviate some of the conflicts which arise as well as facilitate the development process by removing many of the delays which *ad hoc* decision-making frequently involves.

Accommodation and transport are the two major sources of conflict. Development of hotels and other tourist accommodation is often at the expense of residential housing, whether by the conversion or demolition of existing housing stock, by pushing land prices and rates beyond the ability of existing residents to pay or by the loss of amenity. Hall (1970) and Eversley (1977), in particular, comment on the loss of housing stock in London, especially in West London, due to the rapid encroachment of hotels in the late 1960s and early 1970s. Arbel and Pizam (1977) note that luxury hotels are being built in order to give an adequate return on the heavy investments required by high land prices in the centre, and that these are not necessarily what many tourists want. The solution they offer is for medium class hotels to be built in more peripheral locations. In a survey of tourists in Tel Aviv, they found that many respondents were prepared to travel 15–20 minutes to the city centre, particularly where sufficient public transport exists. Eversley (1977) argues, however, that shifting hotels to the suburbs would only make the problem more acute as densities there would need to be lower and thus the demands on space higher. A co-ordinated city plan could perhaps balance hotel needs with new housing projects or incorporate hotel developments in urban renewal operations, as many inner city areas have long been depopulating for a variety of other reasons. Attempts could also be made to increase year-round occupancy thereby accommodating more tourists without increasing space demands. Urban areas have a greater potential for this than many resorts as the seasonality component in their attractions is inherently much less pronounced.

Development of other forms of accommodation could also shift the pressure away from the city centre. Many motels, for example, locate on major access routes, as they serve mainly motoring holiday-makers. Also their lower densities do not allow them to support the more expensive central sites. New Zealand planning regulations have been mainly concerned with restrictions on densities and with ensuring adequate access and off-street parking. Most New Zealand local authorities appear to consider motels as compatible with other uses in residential zones, being comparable to multi-unit dwellings, although zoning has been enforced in some cities (Grant, 1974). In Tauranga, for example, motels have been restricted to properties fronting major traffic routes. The clustering of motels in such locations also assists motorists to find a motel more readily, particularly if they have not reserved in advance. Other motels may locate near particular attractions, for example, close to major recreational facilities, and planning provision must be made for these as well.

The concentration of accommodation and attractions in a few localities can quickly lead to or increase traffic congestion, especially as many inner-city areas already experience heavy traffic flows. Additional pressure from tourist traffic may have hastened the move towards the creation of pedestrian malls in some European cities. Pedestrianization coupled with adequate nearby parking or at least the provision of unloading zones for tour buses and the promotion of special public transport passes or even the introduction of special shuttle services, may ease some of the pressure in other cities (Schaer, 1978). Many constraints remain nevertheless. The majority of attractions are fixed in space and promotion of suburban attractions, at least in London, has been markedly unsuccessful in altering tourist flows (Eversley, 1977). The timing of other attractions, such as the Changing of the Guard, may also be fixed, giving little possibility for scheduling traffic. Again, a basic starting point for the problem will often be the explicit recognition of the nature and demands of tourist traffic in any master transportation plan.

Historic towns

The problems faced by historic towns will be similar to those of other urban centres but certain conflicts may be heightened by the form of those towns and the need to preserve their existing fabric, the basis of the towns' attractions. Inner city congestion will be increased in many older cities by street patterns which are ill-adapted to vehicular traffic. Extra care must be taken with the construction of tourist facilities such as hotels, to reduce contrasts in style between the new and the old. Maintenance of existing buildings and features may be particularly expensive. The focus for development will be the existing buildings and street lay-out which must be inventoried and studied carefully (UN 1970; Solesbury, 1976; Newcomb, 1979). Solesbury sees strategies for reconciling conservation and tourism involving three components:

(a) preservation of the existing fabric;
(b) the adoption of management rather than development policies for making better use of existing tourist facilities;
(c) restrictions on visitor numbers.

Many historic buildings or façades in European cities and elsewhere are protected by local authority legislation whereby strict building codes do not permit deviations from the traditional style. Such policies may be expensive but the increased revenue from tourism may provide their economic justification. Conversion of buildings to new tourist purposes while retaining their traditional form may be another direct contribution of the tourist industry. Newcomb (1979) also cites the case of the harbour district of Ilsvikora in Trondheim, Norway, where modernization and preservation of the existing housing stock was shown to be cheaper than demolition and replacement. However, successful restoration may inflate property values and rents to the extent that existing tenants are no longer able to afford to stay in their homes (Kain, 1978–79). Control and management of traffic is especially important in historic towns. As Solesbury (1976) notes, in addition to amenity loss through congestion, old buildings are threatened directly by impact and more insidiously through exhaust emissions and vibration. The creation of pedestrian precincts appears a particularly appropriate solution for historic towns where the prime purpose for tourists is sightseeing. Where the attractions are concentrated, this can be successfully accomplished on foot as cities such as Bruges and Venice, with natural constraints on vehicular traffic, have shown. However, attempts in Victoria, British Columbia, to redirect pedestrian traffic by the creation of pathways and to hold it in particular parts of the city through the development of open spaces and retail nodes has met with only limited success (Murphy, 1980). Other strategies encourage non-essential traffic away from the city centre, as at Oxford and Chester where one-way street systems have been introduced. Solesbury also advocates reducing pressure by promoting alternative attractions and encouraging a more even spread of the tourist traffic throughout the year. Planning and management of historic towns is more complicated where there are competing land uses (English Tourist Board, n.d.) but where the sole functions are preservation and tourism, more sophisticated techniques can be employed. In Virginia's Colonial Williamsburg, for instance, there is a careful 'processing' and scheduling of visitors, the principal streets are closed to cars and buses except non-diesel shuttles and extra facilities are provided in summer when advertising is virtually abandoned (McCaskey, 1975). Other means for preserving and developing the past outside urban areas are discussed by Newcomb (1979).).

CONSTRAINTS ON PLANNING

In addition to the difficulties discussed earlier, those planning for tourism may be faced with a number of other problems and constraints. Data shortages and a lack of trained personnel are common, especially in developing countries. One consequence of this may be the imitation of existing models of development and consumption which may be inappropriate for a particular situation. The specific characteristics of the development area must be taken into account. Difficulties may also arise between the formulation of a plan and its implementation. Too often plans lack effective legal means of enforcement, or even where they are indicative in nature fiscal incentives may be insufficient or the plans may be couched in such terms that they are not readily understood and thus accepted by decision-makers, developers or the public at large. Vukonic et al., (1978) note that physical plans for tourism in Yugoslavia are only informal legal and technical documents. Their implementation depends on smaller scale urban plans which are often changed by local authorities motivated more by short-term interests than long-term considerations. Thus tourism plans may be prepared but not subsequently realized. Co-ordination between the different levels of government would appear to be a major problem, particularly where national governments formulate the plans but do not offer the resources to the local authorities to implement them.

Even where development follows the formulation of a plan the planning process is not complete. As Kahnert (1976) observes: 'a plan is static and planning must be dynamic'. Flexibility is needed to meet changing conditions; for example, the energy crisis which few predicted and the continuing uncertainties regarding oil supplies. Plans and developments must therefore be carefully monitored, both to ensure that the plan as established is followed or is adapted where necessary to meet new demands. Feed-back systems conveying the results of monitoring are incorporated into the planning processes advocated by Baretje (1973) and by Lawson and Baud-Bovy (1977).

CONCLUSIONS

This chapter has shown how planning draws together many of the factors discussed in earlier chapters. Much spatial planning at the local level concerns the organization of the factors outlined in Chapter 2. At all levels, especially the regional and national levels, co-ordination of major public infrastructure with the goals and needs of private enterprise is important. The ability to evaluate regions and sites for tourist development using the techniques reviewed in Chapter 3 becomes essential when deciding priorities, allocating resources and devising development strategies. Planning at all levels can also help to maximize the economic, social and environmental benefits which tourism may bring and at the same time reduce many of the associated costs discussed in Chapter 4. The emphasis here has been on spatial planning but this must also be seen in the context of an overall planning process, as outlined in the case of the Thai National Plan and discussed in the Languedoc-Roussillon operation described in the following chapter.

CHAPTER 6

QUEENSTOWN AND LANGUEDOC-ROUSSILLON – CONTRASTS IN DEVELOPMENT

Two contrasting case studies have been chosen to draw together many of the themes discussed systematically in earlier chapters – Queenstown and Languedoc-Roussillon. Queenstown provides a New World example of largely unplanned development at the resort level, whereas the operation to develop the Languedoc-Roussillon littoral in southern France is one of the single largest tourist development operations yet undertaken and one characterized by a marked degree of planning and central co-ordination. In each case an attempt is made to set the context and then to relate the nature and extent of impact to the process of development. In Queenstown's case the relationships between the different sectors and agents of development have evolved gradually, largely in response to market conditions, whereas in Languedoc-Roussillon the different roles were defined from the outset. Languedoc-Roussillon also exemplifies many of the principles of planning at the regional level and the place of resource evaluation in this process. Development in Queenstown, on the other hand, has been much more haphazard and planning procedures there have yet to be fully adapted to the tourist industry. To date, development in each area has been reasonably successful but shortcomings are also found, whether with uncontrolled private development or with the centrally planned and co-ordinated operation which has not taken full account of market forces.

Queenstown

In the last three decades, Queenstown, New Zealand, has developed from a regional holiday centre to one of the country's foremost resorts. The first part of this chapter examines the process by which this has occurred and the impact which this expansion has had on the community (borough population, 1,442 in 1976). Queenstown (altitude 329 m) is located 283 km from Dunedin and 187 km from Invercargill, midway along the eastern shore of Lake Wakatipu, the second largest of the southern glacial lakes (Fig. 6.1). Across the lake, the Remarkables rise steeply and majestically to 2,331 m. The resort is favoured by warm, sunny summers (January mean daily maximum temperature 22°C; 1,951 hours of bright sunshine p.a.). Winters are brisk and the rainfall is low (850 mm p.a.). This splendid physical setting and the attractive climate constitute the basis of Queenstown's appeal. To this is added a rich cultural heritage as the town was settled in the early 1860s during the Central Otago goldrushes. Later, it served the needs of the surrounding rural community.

From its earliest days, Queenstown attracted a small number of overseas tourists, mostly those following the itineraries of New Zealand described in the first guide-books.

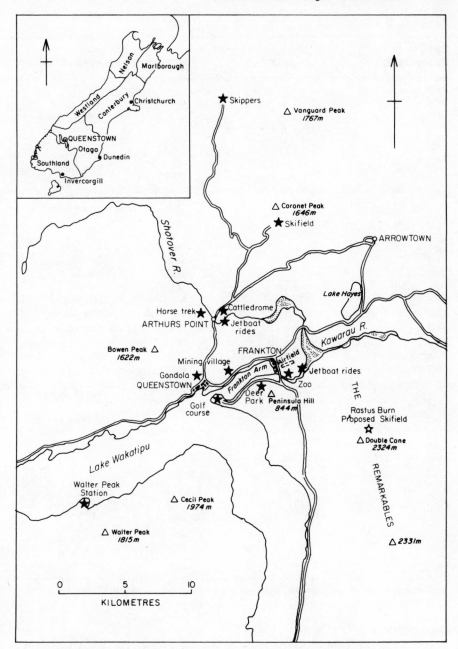

6.1 Queenstown and district.

But accessible from Dunedin and Invercargill by rail and steamer from the 1880s, it attracted many more domestic holidaymakers – 488 excursionists visited Queenstown in February and March 1885 (Ryan, 1971). During the inter-war period domestic tourism grew. The town attracted many campers and a number of holiday homes were built. Most development, however, has occurred since 1950.

Table 6.1 Queenstown: development of facilities (1950–1977)

DATE ESTABLISHED	HOTELS	MOTELS	ATTRACTIONS
1977			
1976		M	
1975	H		Colonial sounds
1974	HH		Cattledrome
1973	H	MM	Kon-Tiki rafts
			Mining village
1972			Back country safari
		MMM	Kawarau jet
1971			Motor museum
		M	Alpine helicopters
1970		MMM	
1969	H	MM	Walter Peak
1968		MM	Goldstream jet
1967		MM	Gondola
1966	H	M	
1965		M	Zoo gardens
1964	HH		Deer park
1963		MM	Shotover jet
1962		M	
1961		M	
1960		M	
1959		M	Moonlight stables
1958			
1957			U-Drive jet boats
1956			
1955			
1954			
1953			
1952			
1951			
1950			Hydrofoil
<1950	HHHH		Coronet peak
			Skippers trip
			Earnslaw

N.B. The table includes only facilities operating at the time of the February 1977 survey.

Development

Table 6.1 summarizes the overall pattern of development in Queenstown since 1950 (Pearce, 1980b). The expansion of the accommodation in the 1960s has been continued into the 1970s, together with a diversification of the attractions and a proliferation of shopping facilities. In addition, the development of package tours and the opening of the Queenstown airport in 1964 have greatly increased the tourist traffic, particularly the number of overseas visitors. New Zealand Tourist and Publicity Department figures suggest the number of visitors has grown from around 106,000 in 1965 to about 180,000 in

EATING HOUSES	ARTS, CRAFTS SOUVENIRS	SHOPS
	XXXXX	S
E	XXX	SSSS
EEE	XXXXX	SSSSSSS
EE		SSSSS
	XX	
E		SSS
	X	
E		SSSS
	X	
		S
		SS
	X	
E		S
	X	SS
E		S
		S
E		
		SS
	X	
		SS
		SSS

1977. During this same period the proportion of overseas visitors nearly doubled from about 20 per cent to 38 per cent (Tourist and Publicity Department, 1967 and 1975). To a certain extent, this increase follows a general growth in overseas visitor arrivals to New Zealand (Pearce, 1977). Australians are the most prominent overseas group in Queenstown. South Island visitors constitute just under half of all visitors to Queenstown (46 per cent in 1974–75) and North Islanders, 16 per cent. A peak of around 8,000 visitors at one time is experienced in January. Significant structural changes have accompanied this expansion.

Accommodation

Motels contributed much of the new bed capacity in the 1960s but the early 1970s saw the construction of large international class hotels (Table 6.2). The motels and hotels differ significantly in their ownership and the markets they serve as well as in the facilities they offer. The development of the hotel sector has been marked by horizontal integration whereby existing hotels have been incorporated into national chains and new chain hotels have been built. Three of the twelve hotels in the district, which together provide a third of the total room capacity, belong to the Vacation chain whose headquarters are now in Auckland. Travelodge, the largest hotel in Queenstown (139 rooms), is operated by the chain of that name, overseas interests holding 40 per cent of its shares (Collins, 1977). It is only the older and smaller hotels which are now independently owned and operated. Upwards of 80 per cent of the guests of the larger hotels are estimated to be from overseas. Many of these are on package tours of New Zealand and spend only one or two nights in Queenstown.

Table 6.2   Distribution of accommodation in Queenstown (1977) Pearce, (1978d)

TYPE	NUMBER	ROOMS/UNITS	BEDS No.	%
Camping ground	4	–	3,000	38.1
Holiday home	445 (x5)	–	2,225	28.3
Hotel	12	673	1,430	18.2
Motel	25	347	1,100	14.0
Youth hostel	1	12	84	1.0
Guest house	3	–	30	0.4
		Total	7,869	100

Structural integration is much less evident in the motel sector where the smaller investments required (Queenstown's motels had an average capital value of $160,000 in 1976) permit more independently owned and operated ventures. Over half of the moteliers came from Southland and Otago. Estimates suggest a far greater variation in the proportion of business drawn from overseas guests (25 per cent to 80 per cent) than is the case for hotels. Few of the motels are large enough to cater for entire tour parties and most appear to cater for the New Zealand holidaymaker or for the overseas visitor travelling independently.

The largest motor camp in Queenstown is owned and managed by the borough council. A second is run by a church and two others are privately operated.

Attractions

The expansion of accommodation has been accompanied by an increase in and diversification of the attractions and recreational facilities provided for the tourist. In particular, there has been an intensification of the trend, noted by Lampen (1968), away from: 'purely scenic excursions to more sophisticated and unusual activities with a peculiarly New Zealand flavour'. In addition to the traditional lake excursions on the steamer Earnslaw and coach trips to Skippers Canyon, there is now a wide range of other outings available by jet-boat, hydrofoil, raft, chairlift, gondola and helicopter. At the same time, the 'staged authenticity' (McCannell, 1973) of the deer park and Walter Peak sheep station have been followed by more sophisticated and more staged attractions; the Golden Terrace Mining Village, Colonial Sounds (a son and lumiére display), the motor museum and the Cattledrome. These attractions have given breadth to Queenstown's appeal but it has been the development of skiing at Coronet Peak which has given depth to the resort. Since the installation of the first rope tow in 1947, facilities at Coronet Peak (1,646 m) have been continually upgraded and expanded to give the resort an important second season (Pearce, 1978b). During the peak of the season, the field handles upwards of 2,000 skiers a day but erratic snowfall has led to the investigation of a second field at Rastus Burn in the Remarkables. There is considerable variation in the foreign clientele of each attraction (30 per cent to 90 per cent).

A mix of large companies and small owner-operators, mainly from the South Island, characterizes ownership in this sector. Some vertical integration is also apparent. The operator of the gondola also owns two motels. Coronet Peak ski-field is operated by the Christchurch-based Mount Cook Lines which has long established tourist transport interests throughout New Zealand (Collins, 1977).

Shops

The retail sector of Queenstown has expanded rapidly in recent years in response to the development of facilities within the town and the growth in the tourist traffic. Almost three quarters of the shops surveyed have been established since 1970. In particular, there has been a proliferation of arts, crafts and souvenir shops since 1974. This expansion coincides with the construction of several new shopping complexes and the opening of the large hotels. Moreover, there has been a general expansion of businesses in Queenstown in the same period, stimulated both by the growing tourist traffic and the increase in personnel required to service it.

The retail sector of Queenstown consists mainly of small, independently owned and operated businesses, the capital required to set up such shops being generally less than that for the other sectors. This is especially so for those whose premises are only leased. Whereas Otago and Southland people are prominent in the general retail sector, the more specialized arts and crafts shops and eating houses tend to be run mainly by extra-regional proprietors.

Overall, the recent development of Queenstown appears to be characterized by a process whereby businesses which depend heavily on overseas visitors tend to be owned by outside companies or by people coming into the area, while those sectors serving a largely New Zealand clientele or local residents (motels, general shops, many attractions) have been developed principally by local or regional interests. In the first case there is a marked contrast between the large chain hotel and the small arts and crafts shop, the former being developed by national companies with professional expertise, the latter often being run by former outsiders attracted primarily by the appeal of the area. While these outside interests have stimulated much of the change, regional participation in the development process remains important.

There has been little concerted effort to plan the growth of tourism in Queenstown. Accommodation appears to have been the leading sector with the increase in hotels and motels resulting from growing external demand giving rise to the development of new attractions and the expansion of the retail sector. However, the borough council, through provisions in the district scheme for land-use zoning, height limitations (12.3 m) and the design and external appearance of buildings, has had some control over the form this development has taken. Not all residents approve though of the size and style of the new hotels. The ribbon development along the lake edge on the approaches to the town is also unfortunate as is the continuing subdivision of Queenstown Hill. Positive steps have been taken however to reduce congestion through the transformation of the main shopping street into a pedestrian mall and the creation of one-way streets. At times the council has

Table 6.3 Employment structure of Queenstown Borough, 1960–77 (Pearce, 1978d).

	QUEENSTOWN				NEW ZEALAND
	1960		1977		1977
	No.	%	No.	%	%
Males					
Wholesale, retail					
restaurants and hotels	35	16.7	285	41.3	15.4
Transport and communication	65	31	116	16.7	11.3
Community and personal services	42	20	121	17.5	19.7
Construction	45	21.4	108	15.6	10.9
Finance, insurance, real					
estate and business services	8	3.8	39	5.6	5.6
Electricity, gas and water	–	–	10	1.5	2.2
Manufacturing	15	7.1	5	0.8	33.3
Forestry and logging	–	–	7	1	1.0
Mining and quarrying	–	–	–	–	0.6
	210	100	691	100	100
Females					
Wholesale, retail					
restaurants and hotels	84	77	328	67.2	21.3
Transport and communication	8	7.3	39	8	6.8
Community and personal services	12	11	77	15.8	
Construction	–	–	5	1	1.2
Finance, insurance, real					
estate and business services	3	2.8	31	6.4	9.2
Electricity, gas and water	–	–	1	0.2	0.5
Manufacturing	2	1.8	6	1.2	24.6
Forestry and logging	–	–	1	0.2	0.1
Mining and quarrying	–	–	–	–	0.1
	109	100	488	100	100
Males in workforce	210	65.8	691	58.6	67.7
Females in workforce	109	34.2	488	41.4	32.3
Total workforce	319		1179		

N.B. Surveyed employment covers all businesses employing two or more persons in all industries except agriculture, hunting, fishing, waterfront work, sea-going work and domestic service in private households. Figures are for April years.

also controlled the rate of expansion, notably by withholding building permits for new hotels in the early 1970s in order to pressure central government into providing financial assistance for a new sewerage scheme.

Impact

No expenditure surveys or detailed economic analyses have yet been carried out in

Queenstown. Other data, however, enable some of the effects of the expansion of the industry to be gauged.

Labour Department figures show that the workforce in Queenstown has more than trebled since 1960, passing from 319 to 1,179 in 1977 (Table 6.3). In particular, many employment opportunities have opened up for women, the number of women in the workforce having quadrupled during this period. As a result, women employees today make up a significantly higher proportion of Queenstown's workforce (41 per cent) than that of the country as a whole (32 per cent). Other structural changes have also occurred. The growth of accommodation and shops has seen a marked increase in the number of males employed in the wholesale, retail, restaurant and hotel sector. This sector has always been the main employer of women although recently there has been some diversification in the demand for female labour. The high percentage of the workforce in this servicing sector stands out markedly against the national average, along with the virtual absence of workers in manufacturing. The above average percentage of workers engaged in transport and communications is a further reflection of Queenstown's function. The numbers involved in construction testify to the continuing growth of the resort. Large numbers of casual workers, including many young Australians, are employed over the peak summer period, particularly in the hotels but also in shops. One hundred and ten staff were employed on the Coronet Peak ski-field in 1976. All but a dozen of these were seasonally employed. The workforce as a whole tends to be extremely mobile but the turnover in casual summer staff is especially great.

Changes in the workforce also appear to have affected the demographic structure of the town. When compared to the national average (Fig. 6.2) Queenstown's population is characterized by· an excess of residents aged 20 to 30, by a short-fall of under 15-year-olds and by a higher proportion of females (53 per cent, cf. 50 per cent for New Zealand).

Heavy demands have been made on Queenstown Borough Council as new infrastructure has been required to meet the growth of the tourist industry (Pearce 1978d). The largest investment has been $1,350,000 for the new sewerage scheme. The borough is also contributing to a new $1,000,000 water supply scheme being undertaken by the

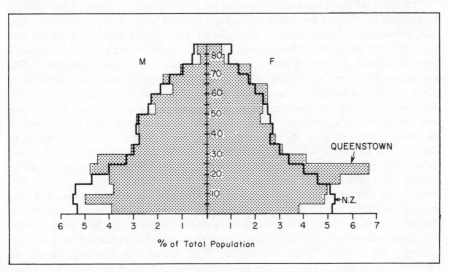

6.2 Age structure of Queenstown borough (1971).

county. Loan repayments and operating costs are largely met through rating (local authority financing). In 1972, the borough reverted to the annual value system of rating, now used by only 5 per cent of local authorities in New Zealand. This is a use-based system rather than a market valuation one and spreads the costs more equitably to the tourist industry (i.e. hotels, motels, restaurants) which now contributes more than half of the rates levied. To further assist the borough council to meet its new commitments, a special Act of Parliament was passed in 1971. This empowered it to develop and sell part of the commonage on Queenstown Hill as building allotments. However, development costs are high and the profits returned to the council are likely to be much lower than originally envisaged. Nevertheless, this is an interesting example of tourism feeding the expansion of tourism. This supplementary income may reduce the mounting public debt resulting from this programme of public works. By 1974, Queenstown's net public debt per head of population was the second highest in the country.

Construction of the new oxidation ponds has removed a major source of environmental stress in the resort for previously, during the peak of the season, effluent was discharged almost directly from the town's septic tanks into the Frankton Arm of Lake Wakatipu. However, the subdivision of the Queenstown Hill commonage itself involves sensitive environmental considerations.

The rating burden was commented on by a number of people in a survey of the attitudes of Queenstown residents to the expansion of tourism (Cant, 1978). Other impacts were also suggested in this survey. While most respondents agreed employment opportunities had improved, the majority also felt that the cost of living had risen as the industry had grown. Property values were also seen to have increased significantly, disadvantaging those seeking rental accommodation or wanting to buy their own home. Unfortunately hard data were not available to compare these trends with those elsewhere. The survey also sought to identify perceived changes in way of life, social relationships and the environment. The general consensus was that the community as a whole had not suffered although different groups or individuals responded differently to particular changes such as a faster pace of life. But, 'all things considered', most households felt they were better off with the expansion of tourism and the changes it had brought.

On the other hand, much public concern has been expressed regarding a new project, the proposal by Mount Cook Lines to develop a ski-field in the Remarkables. Their proposal involves the construction of a 13 km access road and the development of ski-field facilities in the Rastus Burn. Rastus Burn had been selected by the company in the early 1970s as the site was seen to offer a more reliable snow cover than Coronet Peak. The area in question is on Crown Land and an environmental impact report was called for by the Department of Lands and Survey who administer it. This was made public in 1975. The Commission for the Environment received many public submissions on the report which it subsequently found to be inadequate. The major environmental consequence of the proposal was seen to be 'the potentially adverse visual impact of sections of the road'. Concern was also expressed at the potential of ski-field facilities 'to detrimentally affect the natural qualities of the area'. A more substantial environmental impact report from the company was called for and appeared in mid-1977 along with a management study prepared by the Department of Lands and Survey. After studying revised roading and other proposals to reduce any adverse environmental impacts, the Land Settlement Board later in the year granted the company permission to go ahead with the Rastus Burn project subject to stringent environmental constraints. A further series of public hearings were held under the Town and Country Planning Act in May 1979. A year later at another hearing the company was granted approval under special conditions to discharge effluent in Rastus Burn. Thus a decade after the first proposals were made, permission was still being obtained to allow the project to go ahead. No doubt in the process many environmental safeguards have been built into the original proposal, but the delays experienced do suggest existing procedures may not yet be adequate for developing ski-fields or for tourism development in general.

Conclusions

As tourism in Queenstown has developed, extra-regional forces have become more important, both in terms of the market and development agents. Local and regional participation nevertheless remains important. Despite a general lack of planning, the resort has developed in a reasonably orderly and successful fashion though at times progress has been checked by a lack of infrastructure and various costs have been borne by the local population. But as Queenstown has grown, so the need for planning future expansion has become more apparent.

LANGUEDOC-ROUSSILLON

One of the single largest and most ambitious tourist development operations yet undertaken is that to develop the Languedoc-Roussillon littoral in southern France. Begun in the early 1960s, the operation embraces the 180 km of the Mediterranean coastline which stretches from the delta of the Rhone to the Spanish border (Fig. 6.3). Here 400,000 new beds have been programmed and some 800 million francs have been invested in major new infrastructural work. Co-ordinated by a central government mission, the operation also involves the participation of regional and local authorities and the private sector. Emphasis is laid on the spatial aspects of planning and on the roles of the different development agents before an attempt is made to evaluate the project's impact and to assess the success of such a large scale undertaking.

Context and objectives

Compared to France's Mediterranean coast east of the Rhone, that to the west was largely undeveloped before the 1960s (Amouroux, 1960; Vielzeuf, 1968). Until then, the long, sandy coastline of Languedoc-Roussillon supported only a few small resorts, most of which were linked closely to one of the larger cities in the hinterland, i.e. Grau-du-Roi (Nimes), Carnon (Montpellier), Narbonne Plage (Narbonne), etc. Climatically, the whole of France's Mediterranean coastline enjoys a uniformly high number of sunshine hours (2,600–3,000 p.a.), but Languedoc-Roussillon experiences more scorching summers, often violent winds (the Tramontane) and colder, wetter spells in winter, compared to the Côte d'Azur. Moreover, the Alpes Maritimes not only shelter the Côte d'Azur but also provide an interesting backdrop to an already picturesque coastline, where small beaches nestle amongst rocky outcrops. In contrast, the Languedoc plain is flat and rather monotonous although towns such as Arles and Aigues Mortes add cultural interest. The coastline itself, although offering extensive sandy beaches, lacks variety and was fringed with many marshy lagoons (étangs) which provided ideal breeding grounds for mosquitoes, a deterrent for many would-be holidaymakers. Most urban development in the region is some 20–30 km inland. The coast itself was poorly served in terms of roading, water supply, power, telephones and other infrastructure. But although it was less attractive than the Côte d'Azur, compared with other parts of France and Western Europe, Languedoc-Roussillon offered enormous potential for tourist development if infrastructural deficiencies could be overcome. Moreover, the Côte d'Azur itself was becoming saturated.

This potential received concrete recognition in 1961 when central government funds

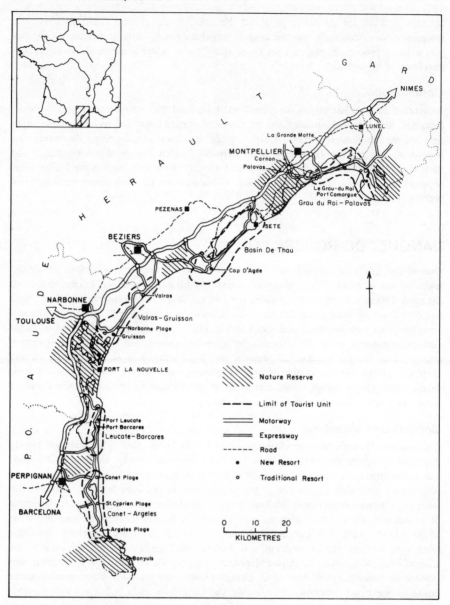

6.3 Languedoc–Roussillon tourist development plan.
(After Mission Interministérielle pour l'Aménagement Touristique du Littoral
Languedoc–Roussillon, *Schéma Directeur, 1972*)

were made available to the regional development commissioner to buy secretly the first
plots of land for the project (Racine, 1969). Following these purchases, a special regional
commission was formally constituted in 1963 (Mission Interministérielle pour l'Aménagement Touristique du Littoral Languedoc-Roussillon) and an official development plan
was elaborated.

The decision to develop Languedoc-Roussillon was essentially an economic one designed to meet both regional and national needs (Racine, 1969; Raynaud, 1969). The region had a lagging economy. It was based largely on monoculture of the vine and production of cheap wine and, as such, subject to many problems (price fluctuations, overseas competition, etc.). Overseas competition had also led to the demise of Roussillon iron ore production and the decline of the textile industries of the foothills (Willis, 1977). Some attempt had been made to broaden the agricultural base of the region by the construction of the Rhône–Sète canal which provided a means of irrigation to grow fresh fruit and market-garden crops but further measures were felt necessary to diversify the regional economy. In any case, the littoral itself was scarcely exploited. The Languedoc-Roussillon plan must also be seen in the context of the country's post-war planning experience (House, 1978) and not in isolation. France's fourth national plan (1962–65) had been broadened to include regional as well as national development. For example, the policy of the 'métropoles d'équilibre,' whereby eight large urban areas were to be developed to counterbalance the growth of Paris, also emerged at this time. No detailed preliminary studies appear to have been undertaken in Languedoc-Roussillon, the absolute size of the operation being sufficient justification, it seems, to ensure it would stimulate the regional economy.

National objectives were also important, perhaps even more so than these regional ones. The balance of payments situation would improve by attracting more foreign tourists and by retaining more French holidaymakers on the nation's coast, rather than seeing them disappear to the Costa Brava or elsewhere abroad. Coupled with this was the State's perceived social responsibility to provide recreational opportunities for its population.

Planning principles

The first plan for the development of the Languedoc-Roussillon littoral appeared in 1964, with modifications being made in 1969 and again in 1972. Although some of the details and names were changed in the process the original principles have been retained (Fig. 6.3). Firstly, it is a comprehensive plan which covers the entire length of the coastline in question and all facets of development. The plan's basic strategy is to concentrate development in five designated tourist units, leaving intermediate areas undeveloped. Such a strategy aims to avoid continuous ribbon development, to protect the more fragile parts of the coast, to bring certain economies of scale (an important consideration given the major infrastructural requirements) and to spread the economic impact evenly throughout the four departments of the region. Each unit incorporates a major new resort of 40,000–50,000 beds, which acts as a development pole, and several smaller existing ones which may be expanded or redeveloped. Development in the easternmost unit, for example, is centred on La Grande Motte (Fig. 6.4). The traditional resorts of Palavas and Le Grau-du-Roi offered little possibility for further expansion but a major redevelopment project for Carnon was undertaken. Later, at the initiative of the Chamber of Commerce of Nimes, a new marina was developed at Port Camargue. The Canet-Angeles unit is an exception, as development there is based on the already established resorts of Canet Plage and St Cyprien. Incorporation of the old and the new broadens the market base, more readily ensures local participation while still permitting new concepts to be developed (see Ch. 5). Of the projected 400,000 new beds, 250,000 are to be built in the new resorts and 150,000 in the existing ones.

Initial selection of the sites for the new resorts, that is by the original 'clandestine' purchases, appears to have been based mainly on the availability of land although other factors such as the need to spread development along the coast and the characteristics of the sites themselves are also apparent. Preference was given to bare or sparsely cultivated

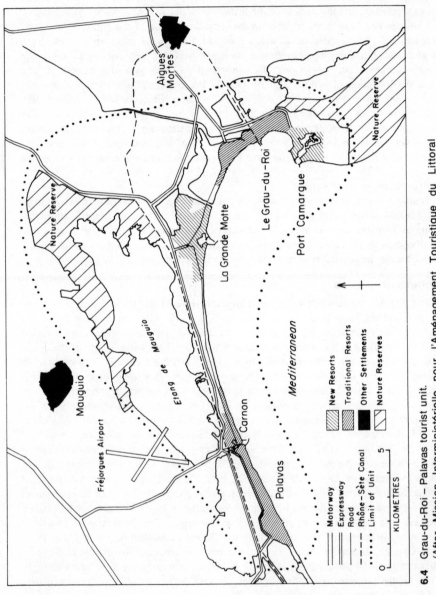

6.4 Grau-du-Roi – Palavas tourist unit.
(After Mission Interministérielle pour l'Aménagement Touristique du Littoral
Languedoc–Roussillon, *Schéma Directeur, 1972*).

land so as not to disrupt existing activity, to obtain the land more cheaply and to give the planners freedom of scope. The State also tried to deal with as few property owners as possible. Most of the 450 hectares for La Grande Motte were obtained from only four landholders. Both here and at Port Barcares, the ready availability of large plots of land appear to have been decisive locating factors. Elsewhere, extreme fragmentation has delayed development, as at Gruissan where 400 hectares were purchased from 450 different owners.

In addition to providing the core for the new resorts, the 1,250 hectares secretly purchased at prevailing low agricultural prices played an important role in the whole operation. The low prices paid served as reference prices for the subsequent purchase of additional land. Such purchases were made possible by the implementation of a 1962 land law, that of the ZAD or zone d'aménagement différé (deferred development zone). Designation of a ZAD gives the State priority in land purchases and freezes land prices. Some 25,000 hectares were declared ZAD's but as insufficient land was obtained from voluntary sales within this area, 5,500 hectares were expropriated by another measure (déclaration d'utilité publique or DUP). On the whole, the policy has been successful and large amounts of land have been rapidly acquired by the State.

Although the coastline was divided up into tourist units, it was also necessary to retain some overall regional coherence. The plan provides for this by the motorway located some distance inland, to which the major resorts are linked by expressways. The motorway provides access throughout the region and a link with the rest of France. This is complemented by the chain of eighteen ports which assures a liaison by sea. Other major operations of a regional nature were those to eradicate the mosquitoes by drainage of marshes and extensive spraying, and to provide shelter belts and create wooded areas through large afforestation projects.

Division of responsibility

A clear and co-ordinated division of responsibility was required to undertake such a large-scale programme. No one organization had the resources or competence to take everything in hand yet the success of the operation depended heavily on all facets of development being carefully co-ordinated. The roles of the State, the local and regional authorities and the private sector were therefore defined right from the outset (Fig. 6.5).

The State. The State was firstly responsible for drawing up the overall development plan. Following this plan it oversees and controls all subsequent phases of the operation through a small but important study team. Secondly, as was noted above, the State acquired all the necessary land for the operation to go ahead as planned. Thirdly, it is responsible for undertaking major infrastructural works; the road network, the ports, afforestation, water supply and much of the mosquito eradication. Finally, State finance is made available to the other authorities to undertake their responsibilities.

Administrative innovations facilitated the work of the State. In 1963 a Mission Interministérielle was created under DATAR (Délégation à l'Aménagement du Territoire et à l'Action Régionale), drawing together representatives of the interested government ministries (finance, interior, development, agriculture and tourism). The Mission is a surprisingly small organization, much of its work being the responsibility of a small study team, consisting of a dozen people. Their role is very much a co-ordinating one, many of the initial studies and most of the actual development work being undertaken by the appropriate government department to which is transferred the necessary finance from the Mission's central budget.

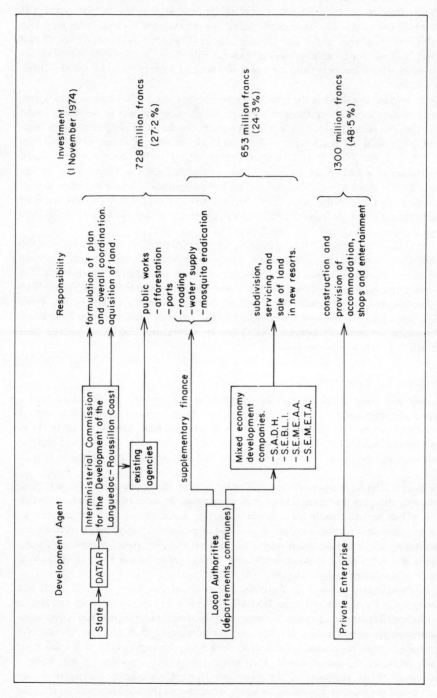

6.5 Division of responsibility in the development of Languedoc–Roussillon.

Local and regional authorities.   The territorial authorities provide supplementary finance for the regional works. They also participate directly in the development of the new resorts through the creation of four mixed-economy companies. The SADH (Société d'Aménagement de l'Hérault), for example, which is responsible for the development of La Grande Motte and Carnon, has as its major shareholders the Département de l'Hérault and three local municipalities. Other shares are held by different government agencies (SCET (Société Centrale pour l'Equipement Touristique); Compagnie Nationale d'Aménagement du Bas-Rhône Languedoc (CNABRL)) and various Chambers of Commerce. Each of the four mixed economy companies is responsible for servicing and developing the land acquired from the State for the major new resorts. Having sub-divided it and installed the necessary services – water, electricity, sewerage, roads, parking areas, telephones – these companies then resell the land at a price to cover initial costs and these improvements to the private sector.

Private sector.   Thus it is only when the plan has been established and the necessary infrastructure undertaken that the private sector enters the development process to construct the hotels, apartments, villas, camping grounds, shops, entertainment and other facilities. Each particular project must conform to the established plan and have the accord of the appropriate chief architect but prices and the decision to sell or let are determined by the individual promoter. Regional firms have played a major role here, particularly in the construction and sale of apartments. Some 60 per cent of apartment construction at La Grande Motte and Carnon and virtually all such development at Port Carmargue has been by promoters from the three local departments of the Gard, Hérault and the Aude. British, German and Japanese capital has been invested in new hotels, a sector which has attracted little interest from the French.

Figure 6.5 also indicates the relative contribution of each of the three development partners during the project's first decade. Whereas the State's projected expenditure is virtually completed, that of the private sector will continue to grow until it may eventually attain a sum equal to twelve times that of the territorial local authorities according to one Mission estimate.

Evaluation and impact

It is now almost two decades since the plan to develop the Languedoc-Roussillon littoral emerged. What has been achieved in that time? The operation can be evaluated from various standpoints although assessment in some instances is limited by a lack of detailed impact studies and in others confused by conflicting figures.

From a technical point of view the operation has been reasonably successful. The unity of direction, the division of responsibility and the comprehensiveness of the operation have brought results. Development has been reasonably orderly and coherent. However, construction has not been as rapid as orginally planned (Table 6.4). La Grande Motte, Port Camargue and Cap d'Agde are now well established but the rhythm of development at Port Leucate, Port Barcares, Gruissan and in the older resorts has been slower than intended. Administrative difficulties arose, for example, at Leucate-Barcares where the new complex straddles the limits of two different departments. The rate of growth also reflects market conditions, for the demand has not always been as strong as initially anticipated. The new resorts themselves present a number of innovations and are very functional in form (see pp. 79–80). Each exhibits a unity of design although this has not always been greeted with universal acceptance (Cazes, 1972).

Although generally well designed and built, critics point to the over-emphasis in these new resorts on private accommodation, that is, on apartments and villas and the corres-

Table 6.4 Construction progress in Languedoc–Roussillon, 1978 (number of beds) (Mission Interministérielle pour l'Aménagement Touristique du Littoral Languedoc–Roussillon)

NEW RESORTS COMMENCEMENT OF CONSTRUCTION	OVERALL PROGRAMME	PROGRAMMES UNDERWAY	
		planned	built
La Grande Motte – 1967	43.763	43.763	30.086
Carnon – 1970	11.300	7.520	3.288
Port-Leucate – 1968	40.300	26.512	11.456
Port-Barcares – 1968	43.323	43.323	17.300
Cap D'Agde – 1970	52.500	35.247	23.870
Gruissan – 1973	42.000	31.925	19.655
Port-Camargue – 1970	20.600	20.600	14.820
Saint-Cyprien –1965	28.000	10.909	3.312
Total	281.786	219.799	123.787

ponding lack of bedspace in hotels, camping grounds, and holiday villages. Although the camping grounds and holiday villages were among the first projects completed at La Grande Motte, thus fulfilling some of the government's declared social objectives, they comprise just on a quarter of the existing bedspace, with most of the future expansion being confined almost entirely to the private sector. Many apartments are rented, but the general lack of uniformity in facilities offered limits their suitability for letting en masse to tour operators. Emphasis on second homes has also exacerbated seasonal problems. In 1974 occupancy rates in the new resorts reached only 71 per cent and 78 per cent respectively for the peak months of July and August, falling to 30 per cent and 40 per cent for the shoulder months of June and September. This situation reflects to a certain extent the lack of marketing undertaken, the first attempts to assess demand apparently not being carried out until 1971 when sales fell away. Baretje and Thurot (1975, p. 56) also criticize the absence of a formal selling agent: 'charged with full powers to negotiate . . . in the generating markets with professional associations, carriers, etc . . .'. Attention is now being directed at facilities and activities such as golf and tennis clubs to attract visitors throughout the year (Lacaze, 1977). Certainly, to date, projects aimed at specific segments of the market, such as the marinas at Port Camargue and especially the nudist colony at Cap d'Agde, have met with marked success.

Despite these problems there has been a significant increase in the number of tourists holidaying on the Languedoc-Roussillon coast. The number of bednights has more than doubled in the period 1968–79, passing from 16 million to 39 million. In excess of 1.6 million tourists are now estimated to stay in the region each summer (Dhivert, 1978). Stays in holiday camps increased by about 600 per cent in this period but the demand for this sort of social facility still exceeds supply. The new resorts are also attracting more and more foreign tourists. In 1974 foreigners spent 5.2 per cent of the bednights for the coast as a whole but 12 per cent for the new resorts (Cap d'Agde 20 per cent, La Grande Motte 10 per cent, Port Camargue 6 per cent). These figures suggest that some of the national objectives of the programme are being met.

In terms of regional development the operation has had mixed results. While the State has spent large sums on buying land, due to the preemptive rights exercised only the prevailing agricultural prices were paid so that no large gains were made by individual property-holders. All land speculation has not been avoided, especially in the immediate hinterland where tourism has dislocated the local agricultural economy by forcing up land values in areas not subject to government controls (Cazes, 1972). The government's policy did, however, enable the operation to be launched successfully although some would argue the inequity of the land purchases given the subsequent property speculation amongst the promoters who acquired the serviced land at such reasonable prices. However, a significant proportion of the promoters are from within the region, particularly in resorts such as Port Camargue, where the local chamber of commerce took the initiative, and in the re-developed resorts. To a certain extent, this merely represents an intra-regional transfer of funds as about a third of those buying dwellings in the new resorts come from Languedoc-Roussillon. Because of the rate of development, many of the public works projects were undertaken by large extra-regional contractors but much of the labour force for the construction of the new resorts came from within the region (Vielzeuf, 1968). In total, the operation is estimated to have created 16,300 permanent jobs (including 7,200 in construction) and 18,700 temporary ones (Lacaze, 1977). Most of the permanent workforce is local in origin, although many of the temporary jobs are filled by students and migrant workers. Despite this, Languedoc-Roussillon continues to record one of the highest unemployment rates in France.

Detailed studies have yet to be undertaken to determine who benefits most from the tourists' spending, estimated to total 1,800 million francs for the four summer months of 1977. In any event, the State has apparently already recovered its initial expenditure through VAT returns on other investments in the operations (Lacaze, 1977). There is little evidence of local authority indebtedness, but some administrative changes have occurred, for example at La Grande Motte, where a new commune has been created on land ceded from the existing commune of Mauguio which was unwilling to become heavily involved in the new tourist activity.

In terms of regional development, a significant policy change came in 1976 when the Mission was authorized to extend its activities away from the littoral to the hinterland. With the exception of the Méjannes-le-Clap project, the objective here is to promote small schemes drawn up by the local bodies. In addition, the SADH, which developed La Grande Motte, has extended its interests to include urban and tourist projects for Sète, a handicraft and housing programme for Pezenas and an industrial zone for Lunel.

1976 also saw a reinforcement of the government's policy to protect the coastline and further measures were taken to ensure certain key zones remained or became public land. The conservation policy to date has been successful and a slowing of demand should mean reserved areas are not brought under pressure in the near future. The orderly development of infrastructure has avoided many of the problems associated with the generation of new wastes. Most of the environmental changes have been brought about by permanent restructuring in terms of the new roading, accommodation and drainage of the marshes. The mosquito eradication campaign has been successful though few studies on the full ecological implications of these changes appear to have been undertaken. Construction of accommodation in terms of the carrying capacities of the beaches has limited the impact of visitors on these (see pp. 36–37).

Conclusions

On the whole, the Languedoc-Roussillon operation has been a technical success. Development has been on a large scale with significant results achieved in terms of provision of plant and infrastructure and environmental management. Commercially, however, results have been less than anticipated and social demands have not been fully met although visitor numbers have increased quite markedly. Clearly there is a need for more marketing studies to match supply with demand. The effects on the regional economy, although yet to be fully measured, appear not to be as great as originally envisaged and the region continues to face high unemployment and other economic problems. In terms of scale and scope the operation is very much a product of its time, with recent changes again reflecting changing administration preferences.

Many opportunities exist for such research. The need to further understand the impacts of tourist development and the necessity for more adequate planning of the tourist industry are only two of the areas in which geographers may contribute. As tourism continues to expand, the demands for more and better knowledge based on sound research will increase.

CONCLUSIONS

The organization of this book derives from the complex, composite character of tourism and the underlying belief that a systematic approach is particularly appropriate for the study of tourist development. The emphasis in Chapters 2 to 4 has been on identifying particular elements, showing the relationships between them and examining associated methodological problems. This progressive unravelling of the various elements of tourist development is followed in Chapters 5 and 6 by syntheses which draw the various strands back together.

Thus after the introductory chapter, Chapter 2 sets the scene by examining the structures and processes of tourist development. Five basic sectors and the different agents of development are outlined then drawn together in a review of various typologies of tourist development. The value of these typologies, it is suggested, lies not only in the specific classifications given but also in the frameworks that their criteria provide for examining tourist development elsewhere. Likewise in Chapter 3 the various locational factors influencing tourist development are identified and then brought together, firstly in a review of evaluation techniques and secondly in a discussion of ski-field location. The complexity of some tourism issues is even more evident in the review of tourist impact in Chapter 4. Here it becomes particularly important to set out the various types of impact which may occur, going from the general to the increasingly specific. At the same time this chapter highlights the need to weigh each type of impact – environmental, social, economic – against the others and to relate particular impacts to specific types of development and the contexts in which they occur.

Chapter 5, which deals with spatial planning for tourism, represents a first synthesis of much of the earlier material. Planning brings together the sectors and development agents of Chapter 2, relies on the evaluation techniques of Chapter 3 and aims at maximizing the benefits and minimizing the costs outlined in Chapter 4. A fuller synthesis, although at a more localized level, is provided with the two more detailed case studies discussed in Chapter 6.

It is also intended that these case studies serve as examples, showing the reader how the frameworks and techniques presented in the preceding chapters can be applied to particular problems. After all, the applied researcher will usually be concerned with a specific development or problem rather than with questions of a general nature. While no text can embrace all possible situations it is hoped that the systematic approach used here will enable the reader in a given situation to identify the relevant factors, to appreciate the ways in which these may interact and to understand some of the methodologies which may be useful. In addressing his particular problem, the reader should especially keep in mind both the composite nature of tourist development and the importance of taking into account local conditions and characteristics.

REFERENCES

ACAU (Atelier Cooperatif d'Architecture et d'Urbanisme) (1976) *Contribution à l'Etude des Programmes de Nouvelles Stations de Vacances.* Les Cahiers du Tourisme, C-7, CHET, Aix-en-Provence.

AIEST (Association Internationale d'Experts Scientifiques du Tourisme) (1978) *Tourism Planning for the Eighties,* Editions AIEST, Berne.

Amouroux, A. (1960) Valras, étude d'une station touristique du Languedoc Méditerranéen, *Mediterranee,* **1**(1), 67–91.

An Foras Forbartha (1970) *Planning for Amenity, Recreation and Tourism,* An Foras Forbartha, Dublin.

An Foras Forbartha (1973) *Brittas Bay: a planning and conservation study,* An Foras Forbartha, Dublin.

Andric, N. *et al.* (1962) Aspects regionaux de la planification touristique, *Tourist Review,* **17**(4), 230–6.

Arbel, A. and **Pizam, A.** (1977) Some determinants of urban hotel location: the tourists' inclinations, *J. Travel Research,* **15**(3), 18–22.

Archer, B. (1973) *The Impact of Domestic Tourism,* Bangor Occasional Papers in Economics No. 2, Univ. Wales Press, Bangor.

Archer, B. (1977) *Tourism Multipliers: the state of the art,* Bangor Occasional Papers in Economics No. 11, University of Wales Press, Bangor.

Archer, B. and **Shea, S.** (1973) *Gravity Models and Tourist Research,* Tourist Research Paper TUR 2, Economics Research Unit, Bangor.

Baiderin, V.V. (1978) Effect of winter recreation on the soil and vegetation of slopes in the vicinity of Kazan, *Soviet J. of Ecology,* **9**(1), 76–86.

Barbaza, Y. (1970) Trois types d'intervention du tourisme dans l'organisation de l'espace littoral, *Annales de Geographie,* **434**, 446–69.

Barbier, B. (1977) Les residences secondaires et l'espace rural français, *Norois,* **96**, 5–8.

Baretje, R. (1973) *Besoins de détente en tant que facteurs pour le developpement regional et agricole.* Informations Internes sur l'Agriculture, No. 116, Commission des Communautés Europeenes.

Baretje, R. (1977) *Tourist Carrying Capacity: essai bibliographique.* Essais, No. 11, Centre des Hautes Etudes Touristiques, Aix-en-Provence.

Baretje, R. and **Defert, P.P.** (1972) *Aspects Economiques du Tourisme,* Berger-Levrault, Paris.

Baretje, R. and **Thurot, J.-M.** (1975) Réflexions sur l'aménagement touristique du Languedoc-Roussillon, *Economie et Humanisme,* **226**, 52–63.

Barkham, J.P. (1973) Recreational carrying capacity: a problem of perception, *Area,* **5**, 218–22.

Bayfield, N.G. (1974) Burial of vegetation by erosion material near chairlifts on Cairngorm, *Biological Conservation,* **6**, 246–51.

Bell, M. (1977) The spatial distribution of second homes: a modified gravity model, *J. Leisure Research,* **9**(3), 225–32.

Besancenot, J.P., Mounier, J. and **de Lavenne, F.** (1978) Les conditions climatiques du tourisme littoral: une methode de recherche compréhensive, *Norois,* **99**, 357–82.

Boaglio, M. (1973) *Tourisme et Développement Economique en Espagne,* La Documentation Francaise, Notes et Etudes Documentaires, 4048, Paris.

Britton, S.B. (1980) A conceptual model of tourism in a peripheral economy, pp. 1–12 in Pearce, D.G. (ed.), *Tourism in the South Pacific: the contribution of research to development and planning*, N.Z. MAB Report No. 6. N.Z. National Commission for Unesco/Dept of Geography, University of Canterbury, Christchurch.
Brown, R.M. (1935) The business of recreation, *Geographical Review*, **25**, 467–75.
Bryden, J. (1973) *Tourism and Development: a case study of the Commonwealth Caribbean*, Cambridge University Press, New York.
Burnet, L. (1963) *Villégiature et Tourisme sur les Cotes de France*, Hachette, Paris.
Cals, J. (1974) *Turismo y Politica Turistica en España: una aproximacion*, Editorial Ariel, Barcelona.
Campagnoli-Ciaccio, C. (1975) Dévelopment touristique et groupes de pression en Sicile, *Travaux de l'Institut de Geographie de Reims*, **23**–4, 81–7.
Cant, R.G. (1978) *Tourism in Queenstown: an invitation to dialogue*, Department of Geography, University of Canterbury, Christchurch.
Carlson, A.S. (1938) Recreation industry of New Hampshire, *Economic Geography*, **14**, 255–70.
Carter, R. (1977) Tourism policy and regional development in Scotland, pp. 31–6, in B.S. Duffield (ed.), *Tourism, a tool for regional development*, Leisure Studies Association, Edinburgh.
Carvajal, B. and **Patri, J.** (1979) Principios basicos para la obtención de un indice de jerarquizacion turistica, aplicado a la provincia Antartica Chilena, *Inform. geogr. Chile*, **26**, 65–80.
Cazes, G. (1972) Réflexions sur l'amenagement touristique du littoral du Languedoc-Roussillon, *L'Espace Geographique*, **1**(3), 193–210.
Cazes, G. (1978) Planification touristique et aménagement du territoire – les grandes tendances pour les années 80, pp. 76–88 in *Tourism Planning for the Eighties*, Editions AIEST, Berne.
Chappis, L. (1974) La montagne, ou en est-on?, *Urbanisme*, **145**, 54–5.
Christaller, W. (1954) Beitrage zu einer Geographie des Fremdenverkehrs, *Erdkunde*, **9**(1), 1–19.
Christaller, W. (1964) Some considerations of tourism location in Europe, *Papers, Regional Science Association*, 95–105.
Clement, H.G. (1961) *The Future of Tourism in the Pacific and Far East*, Checchi and Co., Washington DC.
Cohen, E. (1972) Toward a sociology of international tourism, *Social Research*, **39**, 164–82.
Cohen, E. (1974) Who is a tourist?, *Sociological Review*, **22**(4), 527–53.
Cohen, E. (1978) Impact of tourism on the physical environment, *Annals of Tourism Research*, **5**(2), 215–37.
Collins, C.O. (1979) Site and situation strategy in tourism planning: a Mexican case study, *Annals of Tourism Research*, **6**(3), 351–66.
Collins, N.J. (1977) *Integration in New Zealand's Tourist Industry*, M.A. thesis (unpublished), Department of Geography, University of Canterbury, Christchurch.
Coppock, J.T. (ed.) (1977) *Second Homes: curse or blessing?*, Pergamon, London.
Crowe, R.B. (1975) Recreation, tourism and climate – a Canadian perspective, *Weather*, **30**(8), 248–54.
Crozier, M.J., Marx, S.L. and **Grant, I.J.** (1978) Off-road vehicle recreation: the impact of off-road motorcycles on soil and vegetation conditions, pp. 76–9, *Proc. 9th N.Z. Geog. Conf.*, N.Z. Geog. Soc., Dunedin.
Cumin, G. (1966) Capacité du domaine skiable, *Economie et Prospective de la Montagne*, 7, 20–4.
Cumin, G. (1970) Les stations intégrées, *Urbanisme*, **116**, 50–3.
de Kadt, E. (1979) *Tourism: passport to development?*, Oxford University Press, Oxford.
Dale, D. and **Weaver, T.** (1974) Trampling effects on vegetation of the trail corridors of north Rocky Mountain forests, *J. Applied Ecology*, **11**, 767–72.
Dauphine, A. and **Ghilardi, N.** (1978) Essai de bioclimatologie touristique: La Côte d'Azur, *Méditerranée*, **33**(3), 3–15.
Day, E.E.D., McCalla, R.J., Millward, H.A. and **Robinson, B.S.** (1977) *The Climate of Fundy National Park and its Implications for Recreation and Park Management*, Atlantic Region Geographical Series No. 1, Dept of Geography, Saint Mary's University, Halifax.
Deasy, G.F. (1949) The tourist industry in a North Woods county, *Economic Geography*, **25**(2), 240–59.
Defert, P. (1966) Le tourisme: facteur de valorisation regional, *Recherche Sociale*, **3**.
Defert, P. (1972) *Les Ressources et les Activites Touristiques: essai d'integration*, Les Cahiers du Tourisme, C-19, CHET, Aix-en-Provence.
Dhivert, M. (1978) La vie estivale à la Grande Motte, *Bas-Rhône Languedoc*, **88**, 21–30.
Dumas, D. (1975) Evolution demographique récente et développement du tourisme dans la province d'Alicante, Espagne, *Méditerranée*, **21**, 3–22.

Eckbo, G. (1969) The landscape of tourism, *Landscape*, **18**(2), 29–31.

ECE (Economic Commission for Europe) (1976) *Planning and Development of the Tourist Industry in the ECE Region*, United Nations, New York.

Eiselen, E. (1945) The tourist industry of a modern highway, US16 in South Dakota, *Economic Geography*, **21**, 221–30.

Elkan, W. (1975) The relation between tourism and employment in Kenya and Tanzania, *J. Development Studies*, **11**(2), 123–30.

Elmasri, E., Zeitun, M. and Moussa, S. (1978) Egypt – twenty years of planned tourist development, pp. 379–406 in *Tourism Planning for the Eighties*, Editions AIEST, Berne.

English Tourist Board (n.d.) *A Study of Tourism in York*, English Tourist Board, London.

English Tourist Board (1977) *Eastbourne Study*, ETB, London.

Ersek, S. and Duzgunoglu, E. (1976) An approach to physical planning for tourism development in Turkey, pp. 68–76 in ECE, *Planning and Development of the Tourist Industry in the ECE Region*, United Nations, New York.

Eversley, D. (1977) The ganglion of tourism: an unresolvable problem for London?, *London J.*, **3**(2), 186–211.

Farwell, T.A. (1970) Resort planning and development, *Cornell H.R.A. Quarterly*, February, 34–7.

Ferrario, F.F. (1979) The evaluation of tourist resources: an applied methodology, *J. Travel Research*, **17**(3), 18–22 and **17**(4), 24–30.

Figuerola, M. (1976) Turismo de masa y sociologia: el caso español, *Travel Research J.*, 25–38.

Fuster, L.F. (1974) *Teoria y Técnica del Turismo*, 4th Edition, Editoria Nacional, Madrid.

Gearing, C.E., Swart, W.W. and Var, T. (1976) *Planning for Tourism Development: quantitative approaches*, Praeger, New York.

Gearing, C.E. and Var, T. (1977) Site selection problem in touristic feasibility reports, *Tourist Review*, **32**(2), 9–16.

Georgulas, N. (1970) Tourist destination features, *J. Town Planning Institute*, **10**, 442–6.

Gilbert, E.W. (1939) The growth of inland and seaside health resorts in England, *Scottish Geographical Magazine*, **55**, 16–35.

Gilbert, E.W. (1949) The growth of Brighton, *Geographical J.*, **114**, 30–52.

Giraud, G. (1971) Port Grimaud, a French water-town under construction, *Build International*, May/June, 144–7.

Gorman, M. *et al*. (eds) (1977) *Design for Tourism, and ICSID interdesign report*, Pergamon, Oxford.

Graburn, N.H.H. (ed.) (1976) *Ethnic and Tourist Arts: cultural expressions from the Fourth World*, University of California Press, Berkeley and Los Angeles.

Grant, R.H. (1974) *Planning controls for motels*, Diploma of Town Planning Dissertation (unpublished), University of Auckland, Auckland.

Gray, F. and Lowerson, J. (1979) Seaside see-saw, *Geographical Magazine*, **51**(6), 433–38.

Gray, H.P. (1970) *International Travel – International Trade*, D.C. Heath and Company, Lexington.

Greenwood, D.J. (1972) Tourism as an agent of change: a Spanish Basque case, *Ethnology*, **11**, 80–91.

Guermond, Y. (1974) Les inégalités géographiques dans le développement agricole: l'exemple du Morbihan, *Norois*, **81**, 39–63.

Gunn, C.A. (1979) *Tourism Planning*, Crane Rusak, New York.

Guthrie, H.W. (1961) Demand for tourists' goods and services in a world market, *Papers, Regional Science Association*, **7**, 159–75.

Hall, P. (1970) A horizon of hotels, *New Society*, 12 March 1970, 445.

Harker, J. (1973) Estimating the climatic potential for winter recreation, *Trent Student Geographer*, **2**, 38–46.

Haughton, J.H., O'Donoghue, M.J., O'Hagan, J.W. and O'Higgins, M. (1975) *The Economic Significance of Tourism within the European Community*, British Tourist Authority, London.

Henderson, D.M. (1975) *The Economic Impact of Tourism: a case study of greater Tayside*, University of Edinburgh, TRRU, Research report no. 13, Edinburgh.

Hills, T.L. and Lundgren, J. (1977) The impact of tourism in the Caribbean: a methodological study, *Annals of Tourism Research*, **4**(5), 248–67.

House, J.W. (1978) *France: an applied geography*, Methuen, London.

IUOTO (International Union of Official Travel Organisations) (1975) *The Impact of International Tourism on the Economic Development of the Developing Countries*. IUOTO/WTO, Geneva.

Jones, D.R.W. (1978) *Prostitution and Tourism*, paper presented to the Peacesat Conference on the Impact of Tourism Development in the Pacific, mimeo.

Jones, S.B. (1933) Mining and tourist towns in the Canadian Rockies, *Economic Geography*, **9**, 368–78.

Kahnert, F. (1976) Some obstacles to efficient development planning in poor countries, pp. 196–201 in Gearing, Swart and Var (eds), *Planning for Tourism Development: quantitative approaches*, Praeger, New York.

Kain, R. (1978–79) Conservation planning in France: policy and practice in the Marais, Paris, *Urbanism Past and Present*, **7**, 22–34.

Kaiser, C. and **Helber, L.E.** (1978) *Tourism Planning and Development*, CBI Publishing Co., Boston.

Kalogéropoulou, H. and **Rozolis, H.** (1978) Definition de la planification en Grèce, pp. 281–6 in AIEST, *Tourism Planning for the Eighties*, Editions AIEST, Berne.

Keller, P. (1976) Objectives and measures for achieving planned tourist development, pp. 190–8 in ECE, *Planning and Development of the Tourist Industry in the ECE Region*, United Nations, New York.

Keogh, B. (1980) Motivations and the choice decisions of skiers, *Tourist Review*, **35**(1), 18–22.

Kirkpatrick, L.W. and **Reeser, W.K.** (1976) The air pollution carrying capacities of selected Colorado mountain valley ski communities, *J. Air Pollution Control Association*, **26**(10), 992–4.

Klopper, R. (1976) Physical planning and tourism in the Federal Republic of Germany, pp. 50–6 in ECE, *Planning and Development of the Tourist Industry in the ECE Region*, United Nations, New York.

Knafou, R. (1978) *Les Stations Intégrées de Sports d'Hiver des Alpes Françaises*, Masson, Paris.

Krippendorf, J. (1977) *Les Devoreurs des Paysages*, 24 Heures, Lausanne.

Lacaze, J.-P. (1977) L'aménagement touristique du Languedoc-Roussillon, Extrait du *Moniteur des Travaux Publics et du Batiment*, No. 25 du 27 Juin.

Lambiri-Dimaki, J. (1976) Tourism and cultural development: the undermining of a myth, pp. 282–5 in *Les Problèmes de Management dans le Domaine du Tourisme*, Editions Gurten, Berne.

Lampen, R.F. (1968) *Tourism in the Lake Wakatipu Basin*, unpublished M.A. Thesis, University of Otago, Dunedin.

Lanquar, R. and **Raynouard, Y.** (1978) *Le Tourisme Social*, Presses Universitaire de France, Paris.

Lawson, F. and **Baud-Bovy, M.** (1977) *Tourism and Recreation Development*, The Architectural Press, London.

Liddle, M.J. (1975) A selective review of the ecological effects of human trampling on natural ecosystems, *Biological Conservation*, **7**, 17–36.

London, C.C. (1975) *Quality skiing at Aspen, Colorado: a study in recreational carrying capacity*, Occasional Paper No. 14, Institute of Arctic and Alpine Research, Boulder.

Long, F. (1978) Tourism: a development cornerstone that crumbled: a case history from the Caribbean, *CERES*, **11**(5), 43–5.

Lundgren, J.O.J. (1972) The development of tourist travel systems – a metropolitan economic hegemony par excellence, *Jahrbuch für Fremdenverkehr*, 20 Jahrgang, 86–120.

McAllister, D.M. and **Klett, F.R.** (1976) A modified gravity model of regional recreation activity with an application to ski trips, *J. Leisure Research*, **8**(1), 22–34.

McCannell, D. (1973) Staged authenticity: arrangements of social space in tourist settings, *American J. Sociology*, **79**(3), 589–603.

McCaskey, T.G. (1975) Conservation of historic areas – management techniques for tourism in the USA, pp. 151–9, in A.J. Burkart and S. Medlik (eds), *The Management of Tourism*, Heinemann, London.

McMurray, K.D. (1930) The use of land for recreation, *Annals Assn. American Geographers*, **20**, 7–20.

Malamud, B. (1973) Gravity model calibration of tourist travel to Las Vegas, *J. Leisure Research*, **5**(1), 23–33.

Martinelli, M. (1976) Meteorology and ski area development and operation, in *Proceedings 4th National Conference on Fire and Forest Meteorology*, USDA For. Serv. Gen. Tech. Rep RM-32.

Miège, J. (1933) La vie touristique en Savoie, *Revue de Géographie Alpine*, **23**, 749–817 and 1934, **24**, 5–213.

Mings, R.C. (1978a) *Climate and Tourism Development: an annotated bibliography*, Climatological Publications, Bibliography Series No. 4, State Climatologist for Arizona, Tempe.

Mings, R.C. (1978b) Tourist industry development: at the cross roads, *Tourist Review*, **33**(3), 2–5.

Mings, R.C. (1978c) The importance of more research on the impacts of tourism, *Annals of Tourism Research*, **5**(3), 340–4.

Miossec, J.M. (1976) *Eléments pour une Théorie de l'Espace Touristique*, Les Cahiers du Tourisme, C-36, CHET, Aix-en-Provence.

Miossec, J.M. (1977) Un modéle de l'espace touristique, *L'Espace Géographique*, **6**(1), 41–8.

Murphy, P.E. (1980) Tourism management using land use planning and landscape design: The Victoria experience, *Canadian Geographer*, **24**(1), 60–71.

Nayacakalou, R. (1972) Investment for tourism in Fijian land, *Pacific Perspective* **1**(1), 34–37.

Nefedova, V.B., Smirnova, Y.D. and **Schvidchenko, L.G.** (1974) Techniques for the recreational evaluation of an area, *Soviet Geography: Review and Translation*, **15**(8), 507–12.

New Zealand Travel and Holidays Association (1966), Travel Digest: Haere-mai convention (presidential address), NZTHA, Wellington.

Newcomb, R.M. (1979) *Planning the Past*, Dawson, Folkestone and Archon, Hamden.

OAS (Organization of American States) (1978) *Grenada Tourism Development Plan*, Reports and Studies Series No. 26, OAS, Washington.

Odouard, A. (1973) Le tourisme et les Iles Canaries, *Les Cahiers d'Outre-Mer*, **102**, 150–71.

OECD (Organization for Economic Corporation and Development) (1967) *Tourism Development and Economic Growth*, OECD Paris.

Parnell, B.K. (1974) *Aonach Mor: a planning report on the prospect of winter sport development at Fort William*, Dept of Planning, Glasgow School of Art, Glasgow.

Pearce, D.G. (1977) *Le Tourisme en Nouvelle-Zélande*, Les Cahiers du Tourisme, B-24, CHET, Aix-en-Provence.

Pearce, D.G. (1978a) Tourist development: two processes, *Travel Research J.*, 43–51.

Pearce, D.G. (1978b) Ski-field development in New Zealand, pp. 91–4 in *Proc. 9th Geography Conference*, NZ Geog. Soc., Dunedin.

Pearce, D.G. (1978c) Form and function in French resorts, *Annals of Tourism Research*, **5**(1), 142–56.

Pearce, D.G. (1978d) A case study of Queenstown, pp. 23–45 in *Tourism and The Environment*, Department of Lands and Survey, Wellington.

Pearce, D.G. (1979a) Towards a geography of tourism, *Annals of Tourism Research*, **6**(3), 245–72.

Pearce, D.G. (1979b) Land tenure and tourist development: a review. *Proc. 10th Geography Conference*, NZ Geog. Soc., Auckland, 148–50.

Pearce, D.G. (1980a) Tourist development at Mount Cook since 1884, *New Zealand Geographer*, **36**(2), 79–84.

Pearce, D.G. (1980b) Tourism and regional development: a genetic approach, *Annals of Tourism Research*, **7**(1), 69–82.

Peck, J.G. and **Lepie, A.S.** (1977) Tourism and development in three North Carolina coastal towns, pp. 159–72 in Smith, V. (ed.), *Hosts and Guests: the anthropology of tourism*, University of Pennsylvania Press, Philadelphia.

Peppelenbosch, P.G.N. and **Tempelman, G.-J.** (1973) Tourism and the developing countries, *Tijdschrift voor Economische en Social Geografie*, **64**(1), 52–8.

Perret, R. and **Bruère, M.** (1970) Les ports du plaisance du Var, *Bulletin du P.C.M.*, mars, 82–90.

Perrin, H. (1971) *Les Stations de Sports d'Hiver*, Berger-Levrault, Paris.

Peters, M. (1969) *International Tourism: the economics and development of the international tourist trade*, Hutchinson, London.

Philippines Department of Tourism (1976) *Ten-Year Development Plan of the Department of Tourism, 1977–1986*, Department of Tourism, Manila.

Phillips, P.H. (1974) Impact reporting: an incremental approach to environmental planning, pp. 63–7 in *Proc. IGU Reg. Conf./8th NZ Geog. Conf.*, Palmerston North.

Piperoglou, J. (1967) Identification and definition of regions in Greek tourist planning, *Papers, Regional Science Association*, 169–76.

Pizam, A. (1978) Tourism's impacts: the social costs to the destination community as perceived by its residents, *J. Travel Research*, **16**(4), 8–12.

Plog, S.C. (1973) Why destination areas rise and fall in popularity, *Cornell HRA Quarterly*, Nov., 13–16.

Poser, H. (1939) Geographische Studien uber den Fremdenverkehr in Riesengebirge, *Abhandlungen der Gesellschaft der Wissenschaften zu Gottingen*, Dritte Folge, **20**, 1–173.

Potter, A.F. (1978) The methodology of impact analysis, *Town and Country Planning*, **46**(9), 400–4.

Préau, P. (1968) Essai d'une typologie de stations de sports d'hiver dans les Alpes du Nord, *Revue de Géographie Alpine*, **58**(1), 127–40.

Préau, P. (1970) Principe d'analyse des sites en montagne, *Urbanisme*, **116**, 21–5.

Préau, P. (1980) L'intervention des communes dans l'aménagement touristique de la montagne, *Revue de Géographie Alpine*, **68**(1), 59–82.

Priddle, G. and **Kreutzwiser, R.** (1977) Evaluating cottage environments in Ontario, pp. 165–79 in J.T. Coppock (ed.), *Second Homes: curse of blessing?*, Pergamon, Oxford.

Racine, P. (1969) La Mission Interministérielle pour l'aménagement du littoral Languedoc-Roussillon, pp. 55–64 in *Aspects Multidisciplinaires du Développement Régional*, OECD, Paris.

Rajotte, F. (1975) The different travel patterns and spatial framework of recreation and tourism, pp. 43–52 in *Tourism as a Factor in National and Regional Development*, Dept. of Geography, Trent University, Occasional Paper 4, Peterborough.

Raynaud, P. (1969) Une opération d'aménagement du territoire, une expérience administrative, une nouvelle conception d'urbanisme, *Techniques et Architecture*, Nov., 34–5.

Reffay, A. (1974) Alpages et stations de sports d'hiver en Haute Tarentaise, *Revue de Géographie Alpine*, **62**(1), 41–73.

Relph, E. (1976) *Place and Placelessness*, Pion, London.

Renard, J. (1972) Tourisme balnéaire et structures foncières: l'exemple du littoral vendéen, *Norois*, **73**, 67–79.

Rey, M. (1968) Acondicionamiento del terreno apto para el esquí y equilibrio entre la capacidad de la estación y las posibilidades del esquí, pp. 97–112 in *Estaciones para Deportes de Invierno*, Instituto de Estudios Turisticos, Madrid.

Ritchie, J.R. and **Zins, M.** (1978) Culture as determinant of the attractiveness of a tourism region, *Annals of Tourism Research*, **5**(2), 252–67.

Ritter, W. (1975) Recreation and tourism in the Islamic countries, *Ekistics*, **236**, 56–9.

Robertson, R.W. (1977) Second-home decisions: the Australian context, pp. 165–180 in J.T. Coppock (ed.), *Second Homes: curse or blessing?*, Pergamon, Oxford.

Robinson, G.W.S. (1972) The recreation geography of South Asia, *Geographical Review*, **62**(4), 561–72.

Rothman, R.A. (1978) Residents and transients: community reaction to seasonal visitors, *J. Travel Research*, **16**(3), 8–13.

Ryan, S.R. (1971) *The Development of the Tourist Industry in Queenstown*, unpublished M.A. Thesis, University of Otago, Dunedin.

Schaer, U. (1978) Traffic problems in holiday resorts, *Tourist Review*, **33**(2), 9–15.

Selke, A.C. (1936) Geographic aspects of the German tourist trade, *Economic Geography*, **12**, 206–16.

Senftleben, W. (1973) Some aspects of the Indian hill stations: a contribution towards a geography of tourist traffic, *Philippines Geographical J.*, **17**(1), 21–9.

Service d'Etude d'Aménagement Touristique du Littoral (n.d.) *Perspectives d'Aménagement à Long Terme du Littoral Français. Equipement et occupation à vocation touristique du littoral.* Rapport de synthèse, Paris.

Simeral, W.B. (1966) A guide to the appraisal of ski areas, *Valuation*, Sept., 44–61.

Singh, T.V. (1975) *Tourism and Tourist Industry*, New Heights, Delhi.

Smith, V.L. (1977a) Recent research on tourism and culture change, *Annals of Tourism Research*, **4**(3), 129–34.

Smith, V.L. (ed.) (1977b) *Hosts and Guests: the anthropology of tourism*, University of Pennsylvania Press, Philadelphia.

Social Tourism Study Group (1976) *Holidays: the social need*, English Tourist Board, London.

Solesbury, W. (1976) Tourism and conservation in historic towns, pp. 94–100 in ECE, *Planning and Development of the Tourist Industry in the ECE Region*, United Nations, New York.

Stanev, P. (1976) Harmful ecological consequences of the development of the tourist industry and their prevention, pp. 79–82 in ECE, *Planning and Development of the Tourist Industry in the ECE Region*, United Nations, New York.

Stankey, G.H. and **Lime, D.W.** (1973) *Recreational Carrying Capacity: an annotated bibliography*, USDA Forest Service General Technical Report, INT-3, Ogden.

Stansfield, C.A. (1969) Recreational land use patterns within an American seaside resort, *Tourist Review*, **24**(4), 128–36.

Stansfield, C.A. (1973) New Jersey's ski industry: the trend towards market orientation, *J. Travel Research*, **11**(3), 6–10.

Stock, R. (1977a) Political and social contributions of international tourism to the development of Israel, *Annals of Tourism Research*, **5**(special no.), 30–42.

Stock, R. (1977b) Israel's tourist industry development system, *Kidma*, **3**(3), 26–34.

Suzuki, Y. (1967) Tourism in Japan, *Festschrift Leopold G. Scheidl*, Zum 60, Geburtstag, 11, Teil, 204–18.

TDC (Netherlands Institute of Tourism Development Consultants) — SGV — **Na Thalang and Co Ltd** (1976) *National Plan on Tourism Development, Final Report*, Tourist Organization of Thailand, Bangkok.

Theuns, D.L. (1976) Notes on the economic impact of international tourism in developing countries, *Tourist Review*, **31**(3), 2–10.

Thompson, P.T. (1971) *The Use of Mountain Recreational Resources: a comparison of recreation and tourism in the Colorado Rockies and the Swiss Alps*, Graduate School of Business Administration, University of Colorado, Boulder.

Tourism Advisory Council (1978) *Report to the Minister of Tourism*, TAC, Wellington.

Tourist and Publicity Department (1967) *Queenstown Tourist Survey*, Wellington.

Tourist and Publicity Department (1975) *Queenstown Tourist Study 1974/75*, Wellington.

Turner, L. and Ash, J. (1975) *The Golden Hordes: international tourism and the pleasure periphery*, London, Constable.

UN (United Nations) (1970) *Report of the Interregional Seminar on Physical Planning for Tourist Development*, Dubrovnik, Yugoslavia, 19 October–3 November 1970. ST/THO/Ser C/131, United Nations, New York.

UNESCO (United Nations Educational Scientific and Cultural Organization) (1976) The effects of tourism on socio-cultural values, *Annals of Tourism Research*, **4**(2), 74–105.

Usher, M.B., Pitt, M. and de Boer, G. (1974) Recreational pressures in the summer months on a nature reserve on the Yorkshire Coast, England, *Environmental Conservation*, **1**(1), 43–9.

Var, T., Beck, R.A.D. and Loftus, P. (1977) Determination of touristic attractiveness of the touristic areas in British Columbia, *J. Travel Research*, **15**(3), 23–9.

Vedenin, Y.A. and Miroshnichenko, N.N. (1970) Evaluation of the natural environment for recreational purposes, *Soviet Geography: Review and Translation*, **11**(3), 198–208.

Veyret-Verner, G. (1972) De la grande station à la petite ville: l'exemple de Chamonix-Mont Blanc, *Revue de Géographie Alpine*, **60**(2), 285–305.

Vielzeuf, B. (1968) Le tourisme balnéaire en bas-Languedoc, *Bulletin Société Languedocienne de Géographie*, **2**(4), 399–418.

Vukonic, B. *et al.* (1978) Italy and Yugoslavia: a case of two touristically advanced countries, pp. 174–204 in *Tourism Planning for the Eighties*, Editions AIEST, Berne.

Wackermann, G. (1978) Le rôle des collectivités locales dans le developpement touristique d'un espace multinational. Etude comparée de l'Alsace, du Pays de Bade et de la Suisse du Nord Ouest, *Hommes et Terres du Nord*, **1**, 109–12.

Wahab, S., Crampon, L.J. and Rothfield, L.M. (1976) *Tourism Marketing*, Tourism International Press, London.

Wall, G. (1971) Car-owners and holiday activities, pp. 106–7 in Lavery, P. (ed.), *Recreational Geography*, David and Charles, London.

Wall, G. and Wright, C. (1977) *The Environmental Impact of Outdoor Recreation*, Department of Geography Publication Series No. 11, University of Waterloo, Waterloo.

Weaver, J. and Dale, D. (1978) Trampling effects of hikers, motorcycles and horses in meadows and forests, *J. Applied Ecology*, **15**(2), 451–7.

White, P.E. (1974) *The Social Impact of Tourism on Host Communities: a study of language change in Switzerland*, School of Geography Research Paper 9, University of Oxford, Oxford.

Willis, F.R. (1977) Languedoc littoral: tourism as an instrument of regional economic growth, *Growth and Change*, **8**(2), 43–7.

Wolfe, R.I. (1970) Discussion of vacation homes, environmental preferences and spatial behaviour, *J. Leisure Research*, **2**(1), 85–7.

Wolfson, M. (1967) Government's role in tourism development, *Development Digest*, **5**(2), 50–6.

Woodland, D.J. and Hooper, J.N.A. (1977) The effect of human trampling on coral reefs, *Biological Conservation*, **11**, 1–4.

Yamamura, J. (1970) Tourism and recreational developments around Tokyo, pp. 63–72 in *Japanese Cities: a geographical approach*, Special Publication No. 2, Assn. Japanese Geographers, Tokyo.

Yapp, G.A. and McDonald, N.S. (1978) A recreation climate model, *J. Environmental Management*, **7**, 235–52.

Young, G. (1973) *Tourism: blessing or blight?*, Penguin, Harmondsworth.

Zinder, H. (1969) *The Future of Tourism in the Eastern Caribbean*, Zinder and Associates, Washington DC.

INDEX